ISLAM
and Christianity today

By the same author

Islam and the Integration of Society

ISLAM

and Christianity today

A contribution to dialogue

W. Montgomery Watt

Foreword by His Excellency
Shaikh Ahmed Zaki Yamani

Routledge & Kegan Paul
London, Boston, Melbourne and Henley

First published in 1983
by Routledge & Kegan Paul plc
39 Store Street, London WC1E 7DD, England
9 Park Street, Boston, Mass. 02108, USA
464 St Kilda Road, Melbourne,
Victoria 3004, Australia and
Broadway House, Newtown Road,
Henley-on-Thames, Oxon RG9 1EN, England

Set in Press Roman by Hope Services, Abingdon, Oxon
and printed in Great Britain by
Redwood Burn Ltd, Trowbridge, Wiltshire

Library of Congress Cataloging in Publication Data

Watt, M. Montgomery (William Montgomery)
Islam and Christianity today.

Includes bibliographical references and index.
1. Islam – Relations – Christianity. 2. Christianity
and other religions – Islam. I. Title.
BP172.W298 1983 297'.1972 83-10949
ISBN 0-7100-9766-2

Contents

Foreword by His Excellency Shaikh Ahmed Zaki Yamani

This work is a very important addition to the long list of scholarly achievements by Professor W. Montgomery Watt. He perceived the pressing need for a dialogue between Christians and Muslims very early on and his tireless persistence has undoubtedly helped pave the way for the meeting between the followers of the two great religions and enhanced the chances of its ultimate success. The very clear line of thought that has characterized his works, products of a distinguished career as an Islamist and Arabist, is evident in this book, his latest 'contribution to dialogue'.

Professor Watt has done much in the effort to free the Western mentality of the shackles of prejudice and hatred that originated in the hostilities of medieval times and that have for so long blinded the Western world to the merit of trying to understand Islam. In spite of the phenomenal difficulties inherent in attempting to reconcile positions that are generally regarded as irreconcilable he has achieved a high level of open-mindedness. His aspirations to the highest degrees of objectivity are apparent in statements (in earlier works) like: 'I am not a Muslim in the usual sense, though I hope I am a "Muslim" as "one surrendered to God"; but I believe that embedded in the Qur'ān and other expressions of the Islamic vision are vast stores of divine truth from which I and other occidentals have still much to learn'; and 'Islam is certainly a strong contender for the supplying of the basic framework of the one religion of the future.'

In the great debate between Christians and Muslims however, there are areas of fundamental principles where no amount of logical discourse can bring the two sides nearer to each other and where therefore the existence of an impasse must be recognized. Issues like the Trinity, the Divinity of Christ and the Crucifixion so central to Christian beliefs, have no place in the Islamic faith, having been categorically refuted by the Qur'ān, on the authenticity of which there is no discord among Muslims. The discussion in this book of the Crucifixion and the 'salvation' it represents therefore will not be very convincing to the Muslim scholar and the attempt to find real parallels to it in Islam will have dubious prospects of success.

Thus it may be impossible in the present state of awareness of the Christian and Muslim worlds to reconcile their respective understandings of the most controversial points at issue between them. The resolution of this problem will, I believe, be achieved somehow, some time in the future when God in his infinite wisdom wills it. But in the meantime the existence of irreconcilable differences between Muslims and Christians should not preclude a much closer interest by the intelligentsia and the masses of each side in the affairs of the other. In this context we can perhaps benefit from the proverbial wisdom of the old Arabic saying *'Ma la yudraku kulluh, la yutraku kulluh'* (What cannot be achieved in its entirety, must not be abandoned in its entirety).

Once the main differences are set aside, if only temporarily, it will become obvious that there is a vast expanse of human conduct and behaviour in which Christians and Muslims will find they are at one. After all, one's whole life in this world and not only part of it is the stage on which one is tested and it is by a human being's whole conduct that he or she will be judged. Islam's emphasis on how Muslims should behave towards fellow human beings is such that the Prophet Muḥammad (God's peace and blessings be upon him) teaches us that 'Religion is Behaviour (towards others)' (Al Din, Al Muamalah).

I believe that the signs around us today augur well for the future of religion in the world. The resurgence of Islam in various parts of the world and the discontent that is often sensed in the Western world with the increasingly materialistic outlook of society in general indicate clearly, to my mind, the direction in which the Christian and Muslim worlds are heading. I hasten to add that the general return to religious values and standards should not necessarily entail a corresponding return to the polarized position the two sides occupied in the past. In this book, as in much of his earlier writings, Professor Watt has done much to correct the wrong information that existed, particularly in the minds of Christians about Islam. He has suggested approaches to an effective dialogue which reflect much ingenuity and deserve close examination and an opportunity to be put to the test.

In order for the one religion of the future to become a reality what is needed today is for both sides to free themselves of the ingrained prejudices and traditional inhibitions that have impeded their movement towards each other. Thus freed, it will be possible for them to proceed in a comprehensive dialogue that is based on the sound premise of 'mutual recognition'. In the words of the Qur'ān:

> and do not argue with the followers of earlier revelation otherwise than in a most kindly manner – unless it be such of them as are bent on evildoing and say: 'We believe in that which has been bestowed from on high upon us, as well as that which has been bestowed upon you: for our God and your God is one and the same, and it is unto Him that we (all) surrender'.

Ahmad Zaki Yamani

Preface

This book is in some respects a personal statement based on over forty years of the 'inner dialogue' which has necessarily resulted from the fact of being a Christian immersed in Islamic studies. As I came to appreciate the other religion positively, I found I had to ask searching questions about my own beliefs. For example, since the Qur'ānic denial that God can have a son is in one sense obviously true, what does it mean to say that Jesus is the son of God? The process of finding answers goes on continuously. I learnt that one set of answers would satisfy me for a time, but that later the questions had to be reopened.

Before I was involved in the dialogue with Islam I had also been personally involved in the dialogue with scientism, which was widely followed at that time. It soon became clear to me that I could not defend my own beliefs against scientism without also defending Islam. One or two printed comments by Muslims which I have read in recent months suggest that many Muslims with a Western education are similarly facing the dialogue with scientism and other aspects of the contemporary outlook, and that they would be interested in my defence of religious beliefs.

The Christianity discussed in this book is almost exclusively that of the main stream as expressed in the ecumenical creeds, which I fully accept. Biblical quotations are from the Authorized Version with the grammar modernized. Similarly, in respect of Islam, I have been chiefly concerned with the main stream of Sunnite Islam, though I have occasionally used illustrations from other tendencies. I have used my own renderings for quotations from the Qur'ān.

This book is primarily concerned with the doctrinal aspects of the meeting of the two religions, and hardly anything has been said about ethical or other aspects. Ethical aspects, in particular, are so complex that they would require a book to themselves.

Finally I would like to thank the Very Reverend Professor John McIntyre, Edinburgh, for important advice and encouragement at a critical period, and Professor Thérèse-Anne Druart, Washington, and the Reverend Betty Marmura, Toronto, for helpful comments on drafts of the philosophical sections.

Edinburgh, August 1983

Chapter 1

Attitudes and approaches

Although this study is chiefly concerned with the meeting of Islam and Christianity in the present, it is important to look briefly at the way in which contemporary attitudes have been shaped by the past.

I Traditional Islamic attitudes to Christianity

Through the preaching of Muḥammad in the early seventh century AD Islam came into being in a region in which certain Jewish and Christian ideas were circulating. Meccan merchants went regularly to places like Gaza and Damascus in the Byzantine empire, which was Orthodox Christian, and they also had contacts with the Abyssinian or Ethopian empire, which was Monophysite Christian. In Mecca itself there were a few Christian individuals, mostly outsiders, while in Medina, where Muḥammad lived from 622 to 632, some Jewish clan-groups were permanently settled. Soon after Muḥammad began to receive revelations (about 610), his wife's uncle Waraqa, who was well versed in the Christian scriptures (though not necessarily a Christian), confidently expressed the view that the revelation which had come to Muḥammad was identical with that received by Moses; and this doubtless strengthened Muḥammad's conviction that he followed a long line of prophets. In consequence of this and other experiences there was a time when the Muslims regarded the Christians as friends. The Qur'ān (5.82) states:

> You [Muḥammad] will indeed find that the most hostile of men towards the believers are the Jews and the idolaters, and you will indeed find that the most friendly of them to the believers are those who say, 'We are Christians'; that is because among them are priests and monks, and they are not proud.

When he went to Medina, Muḥammad was surprised and dismayed to find that the Jews there, with one or two exceptions, far from regarding him as a prophet, used their knowledge of the Old Testament to criticize his claim to prophethood. In the closing years of his life he appears to have met Christians whose attitude was similar. This led to a change of attitude among the Muslims. Originally the Qur'ān had presented Islam as a religion parallel to Judaism and Christianity and confirming their scriptures.[1] Before long, however, it became necessary to erect 'defences' against Jews and Christians to prevent them disturbing the faith of simple Muslims. The chief point made in the Qur'ān was that Islam is the religion of Abraham in its purity, and that Abraham was neither a Jew nor a Christian, since he had lived before the revelation of the Torah to Moses or the Gospel to Jesus.[2] The Jews and Christians, on the other hand, had deviated from the revelation they had received and had introduced false doctrines, which the Qur'ān explicitly refuted. The Qur'ān uses the word *ḥanīf* for an adherent of this presumed religion of Abraham.

Within a dozen years of Muḥammad's death the Arabs had conquered the provinces of Iraq, Syria and Egypt, and were continuing to expand eastwards and westwards. The conquests brought them into contact with many well-educated Christians, and some further 'defence' became necessary. This took the form of elaborating a doctrine of the 'corruption' (*taḥrīf*) of the Jewish and Christian scriptures.[3] This doctrine was never precisely formulated, and was understood by Muslim writers in various ways. Some thought that the actual text of the Bible had been altered, while others said that it was only the interpretation which had been changed. The doctrine is allegedly based on some verses of the Qur'ān; but on examination these prove to deal with minor matters, or else to be altogether vague, like 2.75 which speaks of 'a party of them [the Jews] hearing the word of God, then 'corrupting' it deliberately after they understood it'. The imprecision of the doctrine did not lessen its usefulness as a 'defence', since if one form was unsuccessful, another could be tried. The net effect of the doctrine was that Christians and Jews were unable to use arguments based on the Bible against Muslims, and instead had to meet them on ground of the Muslims' choosing.

Loosely connected with this doctrine of 'corruption' is another belief, which is not merely a 'defence' but also part of the self-image of Islam. This may be called the belief in the self-sufficiency of Islam, though it has also other aspects. An illustration of it is the story of the caliph 'Umar and the general who had just captured Alexandria. When asked by the general what was to be done with the books in the great library, 'Umar is said to have replied: 'If they are in agreement with the Qur'ān, they are unnecessary and may be destroyed; if they are not in agreement with the Qur'ān, they are dangerous and should certainly be destroyed.' This story is probably not factually true, but it expresses exactly a belief still common among Muslims, namely, that all the religious and moral guidance required by the human race from now to the end of time is to be found in the Qur'ān (coupled with the example of Muḥammad). This belief may go back to the feeling of the nomadic Arab that he was superior to all peasants and city-dwellers and had nothing to learn from them. It was a kind of corollary to the doctrine of the 'corruption' of the scriptures, since, if these contained false assertions, it was better not to read them. It led many medieval Muslim scholars to deny even obvious borrowings from non-Islamic sources, such as the genealogy from Abraham back to Adam found at the beginning of the life of Muḥammad by Ibn-Hishām. In more recent times it has made many Muslims unwilling to learn from the West even when failure to do so was to their own disadvantage. Only in the last decade or so, for example, have any Muslim scholars begun the serious study of other religions.

II Traditional Christian attitudes to Islam

When Greek-speaking Christian theologians learned about Islam, they first of all classified it as a Christian heresy. As their knowledge of it increased, they gave ever fuller accounts of its false assertions, as well as charging Muḥammad with various moral weaknesses.[4] These were their 'defences' against Islam and were particularly necessary for the many groups of eastern Christians who became 'protected minorities' under Muslim rulers. Western Christendom, however, and the West generally, appears to have been little influenced by the work of these Orthodox, Monophysite and Nestorian theologians.

Western Christians had little contact with Muslims until the occupation of Spain in the early eighth century and the conquest of Sicily in the ninth. After this they gradually became aware that in these regions and on the southern coasts of the Mediterranean they had a formidable enemy, who was culturally far superior to them, and whose military might was redoubtable. For some considerable time they had little accurate knowledge of Islam. Mahound, a deformation of the name of the Prophet, was popularly identified with the devil. The Crusades brought a demand for fuller knowledge, and from about 1100 for a century or two this was provided by various scholars. Yet, although they had access to the Qur'ān and other Muslim books, the image of Islam which they produced for Western Europe was a distorted one. This was probably because even the scholars had a feeling of cultural inferiority, and so by way of 'defence' had to show that as a religion Islam was much inferior to Christianity. Among the points which went to compose this 'distorted image' of Islam were the following: Islamic doctrine contained many false assertions and deliberate perversions of the truth; Islam was a religion of violence, spreading by the sword; it was a religion of self-indulgence, especially sexual; and since Muḥammad, besides exhibiting moral weaknesses, was the author of a false religion, he must be a tool or agent of the devil.[5] None of these points could be accepted by an objective historian today. The 'distorted image', however, has continued to influence the Western understanding of Islam into the present century, despite the efforts of scholars for two hundred years or more to correct the more flagrant distortions. Just as their efforts appeared to be successful certain events linked with the present revival of Islam are causing not a few Westerners to turn back to the 'distorted image'.

III The nature of dialogue

One of the distinctive features of the present age is its religious pluralism. Before the nineteenth century there were very few contacts between the members of the great world religions. Even the beginnings of European colonialism did not lead to many close contacts between persons who felt themselves social equals. In the nineteenth and twentieth centuries as communications improved and trade expanded contacts gradually became much more frequent; and since 1950 there has been a considerable acceleration of the process, coupled with world-wide movements of population. It is reckoned that there are now (1983) nearly seven million Muslims in Western Europe, and there are also several millions in North America. Western statesmen have to sit around a table with Muslim statesmen, Western factory-workers find Muslims on the same assembly line, and Western school-children find Muslims among their classmates. This is the contemporary meeting of Islam and Christianity.

Where the relation between members of different religions is a friendly one, it is convenient to speak of 'dialogue'. This can occur in various forms. There may be officially organized meetings such as the 'Seminar of Islamo-Christian Dialogue', held in Tripoli, Libya in February 1976; or neighbours who have become friends may find their conversation turning to religious matters. The Christian scholar engaged in the study of Islam is also in a sense involved in dialogue. Such experiences normally lead those who share in them to reflect deeply on their religious beliefs in the privacy of their own thoughts, since to meet someone with opposing views is disturbing. Reflection may merely confirm some people in an attitude of xenophobia, in which the 'defences' are strengthened. Others, however, may begin to open themselves to the other's truth and so enter into dialogue, for dialogue might be described as the mutual exchange of views between people who have a genuine concern for one another and are open to learn from one another.

An attitude of openness requires a lowering or demolition of 'defences' of the type described above. The great world religions have all erected 'defences' to protect the faith of their adherents from attacks and challenges made by other religious communities with whom they had contacts, or by sectarians or heretics from within their own ranks. A common form of 'defence' is to present the other religion as inferior to one's own in certain ways, and this nearly always involves *mis*-representing it. Examples of this are the Islamic doctrine of the 'corruption' of the Bible and the Christian 'distorted image' of Islam. The cruder misrepresentations cannot survive a few elementary conversations with members of the other religion; but there are other cases where the 'defence' is subtly interwoven with positive assertions about one's own religion which cannot easily be abandoned. It then becomes necessary, if one wants to enter into real dialogue, deliberately to cultivate an attitude of openness. This was well expressed by the Muslim thinker al-Ghazālī (d. 1111) in a passage in which he described his personal attitude in the face of religious pluralism. He wrote:

> I have made an assault on every problem, I have plunged into every abyss, I have scrutinized the creed of every sect, I have tried to lay bare the inmost doctrines of every community; all this I have done with the aim of distinguishing between true and false, between sound tradition and heretical innovation.[6]

The meeting of Islam and Christianity at the present time takes place in a situation in which both—and indeed all other religions—are subject to attack from many quarters; and the Christian who defends his own beliefs against such attacks finds that he is at the same time defending some of the beliefs of his Muslim friend. In the pages that follow most attention is paid to criticisms based on scientism, that is, the system of assumptions and presuppositions, thought to be derived from science and accepted by some scientists, but in fact of dubious validity and no part of science proper. While some of the assumptions of scientism are here refuted, however, the results generally recognized by scientists will be fully accepted. The same will hold of the results and methods of historical and literary criticism. For the discussion of such questions some philosophical basis is necessary, and, since no adequate basis exists in contemporary philosophy, an attempt has been made to create such a basis by bringing together ideas from different quarters and trying to give them some measure of coherence. Among the writers laid under contribution are Pierre Teilhard de Chardin, John Macmurray, Michael Polanyi and Peter Berger.

In the final writing of this book an attempt has been made to go beyond an attitude of mere openness to alien truth in order to find something more positive. Nearly a century and a half ago Thomas Carlyle, speaking about Muḥammad in his lecture on 'The Hero as Prophet', said that in order to get at his secret he intended 'to say all the good of him I justly can'. More recently, Thomas Merton has in effect said that the good Christian is not the one who can refute other religions, but one who can affirm the truth in them and then go further.[7] This thought is adopted here as a guiding principle. It expresses an attitude which is more than ever necessary at the present time when many in the West are trying to reconstruct medieval Christendom's 'defences' by reasserting aspects of the 'distorted image'. Moreover, Merton's principle is not restricted to Christians, but can be adopted and adapted by Muslims and members of other religions. With such an attitude dialogue becomes a process of mutual witnessing. Neither party is abandoning anything of its essential truth (though it may be gaining a clearer idea of what is truly essential), but both are caught up into a friendly rivalry to discover which can show to the other the fullest and deepest truth.

Chapter 2

The affirmation of religious truth against scientism

The purpose of this chapter is to defend the truth of religious assertions in the face of criticisms and doubts current among our contemporaries, especially those which arise from scientism. Part of the process consists in formulating an intellectual or philosophical basis for argument, and this basis will also be used in the more detailed discussions in later chapters.

I The verification of religious truth

(a) The social construction of reality

It is convenient to begin the presentation of the conceptions to be adopted by looking at the sociological theory of 'the social construction of reality' which has been advanced by Peter Berger and Thomas Luckmann.[1] The interest here is in the more elementary parts of the theory, not in such matters as the legitimation of social institutions. While something similar could be found in the works of other thinkers, the Berger-Luckmann formulations contain one or two useful and memorable phrases. Some sentences may be quoted from their account of 'the world of everyday life':

> Everyday life presents itself as a reality interpreted by men and subjectively meaningful to them as a coherent world. . . . The world of everyday life is not only taken for granted as reality by the ordinary members of society in the subjectively meaningful conduct of their lives. It is a world that *originates in their thoughts and actions*, and is maintained as real by these.[2]

These words may be supplemented by two quotations from a later book by Peter Berger, *The Social Reality of Religion.*[3]

> Man's world-building activity is always a collective enterprise. Man's internal appropriation of a world must also take place in a collectivity. It has by now become a social-scientific platitude to say that it is impossible to become or to be human . . . except in society.
>
> The fact of language, even if taken by itself, can readily be seen as the imposition of order upon experience. Language nomizes (*sc.* gives a nomos or meaningful order) by imposing differentiation and structure upon the ongoing flux of experience.

The main point here is that the common sense view of reality is developed by men in association with others in much the same way as they develop language. Indeed it is through the mutuality of language that men learn to characterize objects as 'trees' or 'stones' or 'water', and actions as 'throwing' or 'carrying'. In this way, over a long period of evolutionary time, the world of everyday life was constructed. As this way of regarding the world is transmitted to later generations, it (ideally) comes to be taken for granted and seen as something objective, 'as inevitable, as part and parcel of the universal "nature of things"'.[4] Because this constructed world has a measure of objectivity it has a certain influence over man's life. Man invents a language and then finds that both his speaking and his thinking are dominated by its grammar. Man produces values and discovers that he feels guilt when he contravenes them.[5]

A common sense view of reality is not always, perhaps only seldom, a coherent whole. There may be enclaves, such as dream life, which some societies are unable to fit into their everyday world. There are also cases where separate segments of the world do not fit together closely; even before the nineteenth century science and religion tended to be kept in separate compartments. Nevertheless men normally aim at greater coherence. Peter Berger expressed this by saying that the nomos or meaningful order of a society (in so far as it is taken for granted or accepted as inevitable) is regarded as belonging to the 'nature of things'.[6]

A religious dogmatic system or symbolic structure is also a view of reality. Even when it is originally proclaimed by one man, there is a sense in which it is socially constructed. The prophet's proclamations have to be taken up by his followers, interpreted by them in accordance with their previous conceptions (world-view), and possibly modified over a period of time in the light of experience. This previous world-view varied slightly from region to region, since each local society tended to construct reality with slightly different basic categories. An interesting example of such differences is seen in Leslie Dewart's study of the words used in the Indo-European languages and in Arabic to designate 'being' and 'existence'.[7] Kant in his critical philosophy regarded his *a priori* categories as belonging to the human mind in general, but it may be that they are rather the categories of his Western European mind, and are derived from the common sense view of reality specific to Western Europe. Whatever the common sense view of reality, however, it seems clear that we see the world in terms of it, as Kant maintained. Something similar holds of the perception of religious truth. It is widely recognized by students of comparative religion that the differences between the great world religions depend in part on pre-theological categorial differences derived from their specific cultural backgrounds, and that this fact makes direct comparison difficult. The difficulty is not absent in the comparison of Islam and Christianity, but it is less here than in many other cases and, except at one or two points, can usually be neglected.

(b) Reality and truth

It may be felt that it is inaccurate to speak of 'constructing' a world, in that the world, or at least the non-human part of it, is what it is apart from humanity. Of course, there is no suggestion that we construct rivers, hills, trees or stars. What we construct is a view of the world, or better, a way of seeing the world and the order or pattern in it. To bring order into a flux or welter of experiences one looks in them for patterns with which one is already familiar; and normally one finds such patterns. Even the order or pattern a scientist sees in geological or astronomical phenomena depends on the categories of thinking to which he has become accustomed at the more primitive levels of daily living.

A similar problem arises with the word 'view'. An objector might say: 'You speak of views of reality, but the fact remains that, whatever men say or think about it, reality is what it is.' Now certainly we ascribe an objective character to most of the things in our everyday world; and by this we mean that they are what they are, whether we are looking at them or thinking of them or remaining unaware of them. Indeed the existence of an objective world in this sense is an element in the common sense view of reality that has been massively verified. On the other hand, when the objector said, 'Reality is what it is', that was a human statement about reality. Whenever people think or speak about reality, however objectively they express themselves, these are of necessity human thoughts and human assertions. There can be no awareness or knowledge of reality that is not human awareness or human knowledge. It would appear to be true that 'some things in the everyday world have an objective character'; but this is still a human belief or conviction.

At the common sense level many statements are made which purport to be objective; indeed most common sense statements are of this kind. They may be about trivial incidents of daily life, such as 'John set the table for his mother', or about general matters, such as 'Day and night follow one another in continuous succession.' Despite the objective form, however, there is always implicit something like 'I/we think, assert, believe, . . . that . . . .' The objective form is sometimes given to statements for subjective reasons; a politician, for example, will say 'Our opponents have wasted the taxpayers' money' because he does not want to suggest, by using 'We hold . . .' or 'We know . . .', that this is merely the view of his own party. On the other hand, the objective form is appropriate where one is convinced that the statement is a satisfactory basis for action. Men are so sure that the succession of days can be relied on that some British driving licences are now being issued with precise expiry dates up to fifty years hence. It is to be noted, however, that the statement about day and night, though completely reliable on most parts of the earth's surface, would not describe the experience of men at the South Pole in midsummer or midwinter, nor of cosmonauts nearing the moon.

To speak, then, of views of reality or assertions about reality instead of saying 'X is real' is a matter of emphasis, and in different contexts different emphases may be required. In daily living the emphasis on objectivity is usually appropriate, since it is in the objective world that our actions take place. In a more theoretical context, however, such as the present discussions, it may be helpful to emphasize the aspect of corrigibility by applying to the statement one of the many terms such as 'view' which draw attention to the possibility of human error. In other words, if one is dealing with a situation where someone is aware of or conscious of X, then one may concentrate one's attention either on X or on the awareness (or consciousness).

After these remarks it is possible to deal briefly with the traditional theories of truth – the correspondence theory and the coherence theory. It is attractive to say that a statement is true when it corresponds or agrees with reality or with fact. The difficulty with this is that, since men have no infallible knowledge of reality, they cannot know infallibly when a statement corresponds with reality. The difficulty is greatly lessened, however, by the fact that statements have many degrees of certainty or acceptability. It is then possible to say that a true statement is one which corresponds with what is generally held to be reality. This is roughly what is meant by the alternative formulation using the word 'fact', since 'fact' commonly means a statement or observation about which men are reasonably certain, and is contrasted with a provisional theory. A theory (which *ex hypothesi* is not certain) is verified by facts, here taken to be the kind of observation which any competent observer can make correctly, such as an instrument-reading or a statistical counting of heads.

The coherence theory applies primarily to cases where the statements or assertions are all at about the same level of certainty. Here there are no statements which are more factual and therefore such that the more speculative statements may be said to correspond with them. This state of affairs is possibly found more frequently in historical research than elsewhere. In such research there is, of course, the evidence of primary sources, and this has a different status from the theories based on it. What is in the primary sources, however, is not necessarily itself fact, but often has to be evaluated by the historian; and his evaluations of the sources are thus included in the statements to which the coherence test applies. Ultimately coherence is a quality of the human account of reality rather than of the reality itself, and for this reason it has often been described as a criterion or test of truth and not as a theory of what truth is.

The primary concern of this book is with the reality of our world, with the world as it really is. The position to be adopted is close to that of the correspondence theory, when it is admitted that there are different degrees of certainty or levels of truth. When one is attempting to give a total view of reality, however, it seems pointless to say that reality must correspond with reality. Any total view of reality, of course, must have fitted into it all the truth in the various branches of knowledge. In order to do this a process of evaluation or refinement may sometimes be necessary, and to this it may be relevant to apply the coherence criterion. At other points there may be correspondence between the view of reality and statements at a more basic level. Essentially a total view of reality is an ideal towards which we hope to come nearer. As we do come nearer, we adopt the objective form and say, 'This is (very nearly) reality as it is.' Truth then becomes a knowledge or awareness of reality as it is.

(c) The centrality of action

Implicit in the theory of the social construction of reality is a conception of the centrality of action. Over three centuries ago Descartes made the assertion that thought is central in human life. It is in thinking and in being aware of himself thinking that man is most certain of his own reality. Such is one way of understanding the famous formula, *Cogito, ergo sum*, 'I think, and so I exist.' It is perhaps significant, however, that, even when Descartes committed himself to his great mental experiment, he did not think it right to abandon the ordinary actions of daily life.[8] To this extent he bore witness to the urgency of action and gave some support to the counter-assertion that action is central. One might perhaps say, *Ago, ergo sum*. The most certain thing about me is that I am living; and to live I must act in various ways, such as breathing, eating, meeting other people and earning a living.

A somewhat similar standpoint was expressed by John Macmurray in *The Self as Agent*:

> There is of necessity an interplay, in all human activities, between theory and practice. It is characteristic of Man that he solves his practical problems by taking thought; and all his theoretical activities have their origins, at least, in his practical requirements. That they also find their meaning and their significance in the practical field will command less general assent; yet it is, in my belief, the truth of the matter. . . . The truth or falsity of the theoretical is to be found solely in its reference to the practical.[9]

The action to which this assertion that action is central refers is human action in the fullest sense. It is not the external physical aspect of human activity or even something mainly physical like breathing, but includes every form of deliberate human participation in the multifarious concerns of society. The act described by the words 'Alan kicked the ball into the net and won the cup for the Blues' may sound like a simple physical act, but it is comprehensible only as part of a vast complex of meaning. This context includes Alan's previous experience of football, his co-operation with the rest of the team, the fact that no other goal was scored between Alan's kick and the end of the match, the rules of the game, the popular enthusiasm for football and many other such matters. Indeed, it is only within this context that we know the act as it *really* is.

It must also be emphasized that in normal human beings an act is never an isolated act, but is part of a whole plan or scheme of life, and the individual's plan is in turn part of the structured life of his society. There is, indeed, a whole hierarchical series of decisions governing various areas of the life of individuals and of society. Alan's decision to kick for goal at a particular moment occurred within a context created by his decision to sign on for the Blues and the further decision to play in this match; and these decisions depended on the decision of a group of men to run a team called the Blues and also to let their team play in a series of cup games organized by a wider football association. Such 'governing decisions' are a universal feature of human life. Some control great areas of life, like the decisions of government or the individual's decision to accept a certain job or marry a certain person; such decisions are not irreversible, but may continue to control subordinate decisions for a long period. If a housewife decides to give her family roast lamb for lunch on Sunday, even that involves her in many further decisions connected with purchasing, cooking and serving. The decision to have another cup of tea at breakfast is almost at the simplest level, but one may still drink the tea at a gulp or take it in sips over a quarter of an hour.

There is also some evidence for the centrality of action in the fact that those religions which believe in the Last Judgment, notably Christianity and Islam, hold that the assignment of a man to Heaven or Hell depends to a great extent on the acts he has done or left undone during his life on earth. Similarly, believers in reincarnation hold that the character of each reincarnation depends on conduct in the previous incarnation.

(d) Action as the test of views of reality

In acting a man is (1) responding to the situation in which he finds himself at (or just before) the moment of action, and (2) is taking account of the likely consequences of his action. The situation here is to be understood as the 'external' situation in the sense of what is external to the man's will; he would certainly have to respond to the fact that his doctor had discovered a cancerous growth in his throat. There is also what might be called an 'internal' situation, namely, the context created by the governing decisions he has made in the past and is not at this moment questioning. It seems best, however, not to speak of an 'internal' situation, but to say that the man's action is subject to his past governing decisions. It is essentially the external situation to which he is responding, not these governing decisions.

The extent of the knowledge of the situation which is appropriate in different cases varies enormously. The Prime Minister of an important state may be elaborately briefed before taking some decision. The ordinary person, before crossing a quiet street to post a letter, requires some knowledge of the vehicular traffic; but a rudimentary knowledge suffices (e.g. that there is only one car in sight and that it is going away from him). Whatever the weightiness or triviality of the decision, however, people are often unable to obtain adequate information about the situation in the time available. In such cases, where they are forced to make some decision, they necessarily act on the basis of incomplete knowledge of the situation. Knowledge of the likely consequences of an action may be even more difficult to obtain, since it may depend in part on factors which cannot be known with certainty, such as next month's weather or the freely chosen actions of a number of people.

In all cases, however, a person is bound to act on the basis of the reality (as he understands it) both of the situation and of the likely consequences. If his understanding of these realities is inadequate or mistaken, the actual consequences may be disastrous for him and for others. Thus if Ferdinand finds thick smoke coming into the room when he opens the door, and judges the building to be on fire, and if he further wrongly supposes the window to be six feet from the ground, when in fact it is sixty feet, and so jumps out the window, he may not survive. On the other hand, a 'slight' mistake about the nature of reality may have hardly any adverse consequences; for example, if Ferdinand's window had actually been ten feet from the ground. It may even happen occasionally that some unforeseen factor may counter a mistake and lead to a happy result. In general, however, mistaken views of the reality of the situation and the likely consequences lead to adverse and unsatisfactory results. In short, action is concerned with reality, and reality is not to be trifled with. This might be succinctly expressed by saying that reality is the sphere in which a person acts and in which his acts have consequences.

For some purposes it is more adequate to think of this reality to which we respond as an ongoing process, indeed the ongoing cosmic process. Our action then becomes an intromission into the process, or an interference with it, which affects the process in certain ways, although in other ways it carries on without being affected. The distinction between situation and consequences still applies, but has a measure of fluidity.

It must be emphasized that the reality within which an action takes place is more than a physico-chemical or 'scientific' reality. That reality must certainly be taken account of, but in addition the action must also take account of the structure of social meaning. This is obvious when Alan plays for the Blues in the Cup Final; but it is also true of virtually every human action, since people are always involved in some measure. One hears of a man spending all his days in a room by himself machining metal into certain shapes; but the man is working for an employer, and the employer is in relation to the ultimate users of the pieces of metal produced. If the man in his actions neglects this social context, he will soon be involved in disastrous consequences.

An extreme case may be imagined to illustrate the urgency of some action and the weightiness of the decision about the (theoretical) basis for action. Suppose a man is travelling on foot through desolate country—perhaps the Australian outback—has lost his way, and is starving. He does not know exactly where the nearest human habitation is; it may be twenty or thirty miles away. In this predicament he finds some mushrooms, and has to decide whether they are edible or poisonous. He has only faint memories of pictures of edible mushrooms. If he decides to eat them, and if they really are edible, he has increased his chances of survival; but if they are really poisonous, he will die. On the other hand, if he decides to treat them as poisonous, he has not worsened his position, except that if they really are edible, he has missed an opportunity of gaining nourishment, and so has lessened his chances of survival. In the first case, that is, when he makes edibility his working hypothesis and eats and gains strength, the result shows the hypothesis to have been true.

More generally it may be asserted that the view adopted as a basis for action is shown to be true or is 'verified' when the action based on it is satisfactory, that is, when the consequences are approximately those foreseen. This principle appears to have governed the whole process of the social construction of the everyday world. While knowledge was still scanty, such simple views as people had were made the basis of action. If the result was satisfactory, the views were accepted as true. If the result was unsatisfactory, some other view was taken as the basis of action, or some modification of the original view. Thus gradually there was built up what has here been called the common-sense view of reality. Some aspects of it have been so amply verified over tens or hundreds of thousands of years that they are now seen as inevitable or part of 'the nature of things'; for example, the continuous succession of day and night.

In scientific research a provisional assertion, which has to be tested by experiment or in some other way, is called a 'hypothesis'. In practical living, on the other hand, it is better to call a provisional assertion a 'basis of action', since, despite its provisional character, the agent has to act on it, and his action may involve questions of life and death. Because of the complexity of most situations it is often not a question of the basis of action's being true or false, but of its having a certain degree of adequacy. In general, a hypothesis is usually less complex and belongs in the first place to a purely intellectual sphere.

The account which has just been given of how the common-sense view of reality is developed amounts to saying that, when people commit themselves to a certain basis of action, then this is accepted as true provided it 'works'. Something like this formulation was used by pragmatists at the beginning of the century.[10] The objection was made to the pragmatists that to say that an assertion 'works' is not the same as to say that it is true; and to this objection the pragmatists had no entirely convincing answer. In the present context, however, the objection may be met by asserting that, if the view of reality on which the action is based 'works', that is, if the outcome of the action is roughly what the agent wanted it to be, then the view must correspond with reality and so be true. For example, if the man who found mushrooms acted on the view that they were edible, and if he lived, then they really were edible.

Discussions of verification in the last half-century have mostly been concerned with isolated assertions and single scientific theories. Whole systems of thought, however, may also be verified by considering how they work in practice. Though philosophers can show that the common-sense view of reality requires modification at certain points, it has in general 'worked' successfully over a period of millennia, and, at least for the normal requirements of daily life, has been massively verified. It cannot be proved that the sun will rise tomorrow in the way in which a theorem of Euclid can be proved, but this basis of action has 'worked' so often in the past that no sensible person would think of acting on any other basis. Moreover, not merely has it 'worked', but it is accepted as part of 'the nature of things'.

In a similar way, though less massively, the achievements of science and science-based technology verify the general truth of science as a system of thought. By this last phrase is meant the totality of the assured results of science (as distinct from probable or provisional theories) accepted by the main body of scientists, together with the methods of scientific research employed in particular fields. An outstanding achievement, such as sending men to the moon and bringing them back again, not only verifies particular scientific theories and procedures involved in the operation, but is also evidence for the general validity of scientific methods within their appropriate sphere.

It has to be recognized, however, that when complex systems of thought 'work', they may do so only in some sense or up to a certain point but that in other ways they are untrue or misleading. This is particularly so with the common-sense view of reality and with religious world-views, but the phenomenon is also to be met with in science. Newtonian physics 'worked' up to a point, and so in a certain sphere was, and is, true, although Einstein showed that it did not have the universal truth claimed for it.

Let us now turn, however, to the inadequacies of common-sense views as seen by the philosophers. What the ordinary man thinks of as a table is shown to be 'a family of sense-data' (empiricists) or 'a well connected series of manifestations' (Sartre), while the scientists think of it as an assemblage of molecules, atoms and various subatomic entities. Yet the common-sense view of the table obviously 'works'. The housewife has no difficulty in setting a plate on the table; but, if she had to think all the time of plate-shaped and table-shaped families of sense-data, she would probably become confused. Thus the table as understood by common-sense must somehow agree or correspond with reality.

A more general formulation of this point would be that, where a basis of action 'works', then in the respects relevant to its 'working' it must be true; that is, it must be a view or presentation or awareness of some part or segment of reality as it is. Unfortunately, it is sometimes difficult to express in words what the relevant aspect is.

(e) The verification of religious views of reality

There are no good grounds for supposing that this criterion of seeing whether a theory 'works' in practice does not apply to religious systems of thought. Religion like science has a place for experiment. The

Wayside Pulpit, that medium of the 1920s and 1930s, once carried the message: 'Religion begins as an experiment and ends as an experience.' In other words, religion is something to be 'tried out'. William James and the pragmatists were ridiculed for appearing to say, 'Try believing in God, and you will find that it works and that you feel better.' Yet this is not far removed from the evangelist who says, 'Believe in God's love in Jesus Christ, and you will be saved.'

Many religious people would insist that the difference between religious assertions and scientific hypotheses is that there is nothing tentative about the former; but the difference is more at the level of psychology than of epistemology. It is the evangelist's utter conviction of the truth of what he says that attracts men to accept his message; but an intelligent man is still justified in asking for grounds for thinking that the message is true. It may also be noted that in Christianity and Islam, and indeed also in Judaism, the original message is a group of joyful or kerygmatic assertions, and that these are not moral prescriptions but are about the nature of the reality which constitutes the sphere in which men have to live and act. Where moral prescriptions are associated with kerygmatic assertions, the latter are primary, and the former have only a secondary or subordinate position.

In science it is usually a single assertion which has to be tested by experiment, but in a religion it is the symbolic structure as a whole, since the individual has to commit himself to the religion and base his whole life on its teaching. Paul Tillich distinguished between the verification by experiment practised in science and the 'experiential' type of verification which 'can occur within the life-process itself', though he does not seem to have applied this specifically to religious assertions.[11] This, like the statement that 'religion begins as an experiment and ends as an experience', exemplifies a principle which can be traced back to the Sermon on the Mount, where it is stated that false prophets are to be distinguished (presumably from true prophets) by their 'fruits', that is, the qualities shown in their own lives and those of their followers.[12]

History records cases where people who accepted kerygmatic assertions experienced, as a result of this, a new and superior quality of life. This was certainly true of the early Christians who accepted the assertion that 'Jesus had risen from the dead'. Something similar is true of early Islam. Those men of Mecca who became Muslims in response to Muḥammad's kerygmatic assertions had to face a measure of persecution, but they seem to have felt that their life as Muslims was nevertheless superior in quality, in that it was more meaningful, more in accordance with the realities of the universe. Later, after the emigration (*Hijra*) to Medina, they came to see the overwhelming defeat of the Meccan pagans at Badr as God's vindication of his prophet and were persuaded, despite some continuing difficulties, of the superiority of their new way of life. As Christianity and Islam spread in Asia and Africa, those who adopted one of these religons felt that they were in some respects entering on a 'better' way of life; and even if material benefits were uppermost in the minds of some of them, others were aware of the spiritual benefits.

In a wider perspective it may be claimed that all the great world-religions have enabled their followers to lead tolerable lives, sometimes in circumstances of great hardship. The proof of this is that they have become world-religions; in the regions of the world where each was dominant men knew of nothing better. Judaism enabled its adherents to remain hopeful in the difficult centuries after the return from exile, and also in later periods of great trouble. Hinduism gives men a sense of joy even in the midst of incredible poverty. Islam has made it possible for men to continue living, without losing heart, in the harsh circumscribed conditions of a Saharan oasis. In a certain sense, then, these religions and the other great religions have 'worked'.

It has to be remembered, however, that a religious view, like views of other kinds, when it 'works' and enables people to lead satisfactory lives, is true only in respect of the aspects which are relevant to its 'working'. This point enables one to deal with the difficulties constituted by the differences occurring within 'a' religion. In the earlier periods individual deviants were virtually unknown, since the religious world-view was reached by 'social construction', so that it appeared inevitable and could be questioned only in exceptional circumstances. The more serious problem was that of sectarian movements. These may be regarded as attempts to modify the general world-view of a religion in points where it is unsatisfactory for a particular group. Many such movements last for only a few decades and then fade away. Others last for a much longer period, like Shīʿism in Islam and the schism between Roman Catholic and Greek Orthodox in Christianity. A movement which successfully maintains itself for a long period must in some respects be more satisfactory for the members of the sect-community than the general world-view of the main body. It is usually found that a sect is marked off from the main body by social, economic, ethnic or geographical factors, and that its distinctive doctrines are somehow relevant to the distinguishing factors.

The system of assertions made by a religion covers a vast area of human experience, and not all the assertions are equally relevant to daily living. The 'defences' raised by a religion against the other religions with which it is in contact help to maintain the confidence of its members when they are puzzled by contrary assertions, but have little to do with the satisfactory conduct of daily life. For this purpose the most relevant assertions are the central credal doctrines. The connection of these doctrines with a satisfactory quality of life is not wholly clear; but it is reasonable to think that, in so far as Christianity and Islam have made possible a good quality of life, the doctrinal assertions in which they are roughly agreed have something to do with this success.

There are also difficulties about verification which are related to the personal destinies of individuals. The believer may see himself suffering hardship and poverty, while some unbeliever whom he knows is rich and prosperous. As a verse in a Psalm (73.3) puts it, 'I was envious at the foolish, when I saw the prosperity of the wicked.' The struggle with this problem runs through much of the Old Testament. The sufferings of believers could indeed be attributed to the fact that they had sinned somehow against God, even when they had not been conscious of so doing; and it could also be maintained that the prosperity of the unbelievers was only temporary. Yet such suggestions did not completely solve the problem. Despite a continuing strand of thought which wanted to maintain that the good man always prospered in the end whereas the ungodly and wicked man suffered misfortune, it came to be realized that there was no simple correlation between goodness or piety and prosperity.

This realization finds expression above all in the book of Job. There an extreme case is imagined of the suffering of an upright believer; and the conclusion of the book appears to be that God's ways are inscrutable, though his goodness is not to be doubted. Against his friends Job maintains his innocence; but, when he has been shown the wonders of God's creative power, he acknowledges his ignorance and lack of understanding and says: 'I have heard of you by the hearing of the ear, but now my eye sees you; wherefore I abhor myself and repent in dust and ashes' (42.5f.).

The same problem is raised by the 'temptation' of Jesus, when the devil suggests that no harm will come to him if he flings himself down from a pinnacle of the temple—doubtless a symbolic description of his entering into conflict with the Jewish leaders—and quotes verses from the Psalms (91.11f.) which state that God's angels will preserve the good man from harm. The answer of Jesus was a quotation from Deuteronomy (6.16), 'You shall not tempt the Lord your God', and this in turn refers to an incident in Exodus (17.7), where the Israelites 'tempted the Lord, saying, "Is the Lord among us or not?"'. In effect, then, the answer of Jesus is that whatever happens, even if it is passion and crucifixion, one must go on believing that God controls events in favour of the good man or woman. Thus Christians have come to believe that the sufferings of good men and women may have a place in the purposes of God, and even to see a negative correlation between piety and misfortune, in that the one who gives himself most completely to the service of God may find that this brings suffering upon him, in line with the word of Jesus about 'taking up one's cross'.

Islam also had to deal with this problem. The followers of Muḥammad, like the followers of other prophets, met with persecution and were called upon to show patience. It was also felt sometimes that the carrying out of God's commands was burdensome, and likewise demanded *ṣabr* or patience. Those who remained faithful were in the end rewarded by 'the great success' (*al-fawz al-'aẓīm*)[13] of being assigned to Paradise at the Judgment, but this might perhaps be equated with the attainment of a supremely meaningful life.

Difficult as is this problem of the suffering of good people, it does not disprove the contention that true religious belief is accompanied by a more satisfactory quality of life. For over three thousand years there have been communities based on the acceptance of belief in a transcendent being, God, who was also held to control the course of events, to guide and strengthen human beings, and to judge them. Most of the members of these communities have considered their lives satisfactory, and thus the central kerygmatic assertions have been massively tested in actual living. As for the individual who has to meet misfortunes, hardships and disabilities to a far greater extent than his fellows, he is better able to cope with his destiny if he himself holds fast to his belief in God and lives in a community of believers. Religious belief does not exempt people from the ordinary ills and weaknesses of the human condition. What it does is to enable them to lead meaningful —and therefore satisfactory—lives in the most adverse circumstances. The satisfactory quality of life claimed for the members of a religious community normally includes an adequate level of material wellbeing and harmonious social relationships, but the ultimate criterion of satisfactoriness is that life should be meaningful.

A further difficulty is that in the opinion of some thinkers Christianity today is not in a healthy state. Certainly in Christendom since about 1500 many persons have continued to profess Christianity but have also adopted secular and humanistic beliefs, and have based their practice partly on these. In such circumstances can we say that, if a life is satisfactory, that is because it is based on Christian beliefs? The matter is too complex to be fully discussed here. Thus some persons, while keeping their religion in a separate compartment, as it were, and sharing their social life almost exclusively with fellow-Christians, may experience their life as satisfactory, and may yet seem to an observer to be leading a narrow and self-centred life. The most relevant point would appear to be that many individuals who find their lives satisfactory, especially in the sense of being meaningful, consciously associate this superior quality of life with their Christian belief, and are unwavering in their attachment to it. One might cite the example of Thomas Merton, who in committing himself as fully as possible to the living of a Christian life, though without shutting out his awareness of the secular world, gained an intensely meaningful life, though one where there was suffering and hardship.

A similar difficulty exists in respect of the other world-religions at the present time, because since the later nineteenth century they have been experiencing 'the impact of the West'. In their case also, however, there are countless individuals, who feel that their lives are satisfactory because of their religious belief, and who are firmly committed to their religious community.

The conclusion from all this is that the great religions over a period of centuries have enabled vast numbers of people to lead a satisfactory life. They have been verified in general. This does not mean that each statement of each religion is to be regarded as true in isolation, but that the symbolic system of each religion, taken as a whole, presents a view of reality which is sound in many or most relevant respects. In theory it is possible to hold that during recent decades the circumstances of daily living have changed so radically that the old religious systems have ceased to be relevant; but the case for this is far from being proved, and the possiblity will be neglected here. The fact that there appear to be contradictions between different religious views of reality will be discussed later, and it will be shown that most of these contradictions are entirely or to a large extent only apparent.

In the particular cases of Islam and Christianity to say that they are verified in general implies accepting their central doctrines as true.

These include the belief that God is one and eternal and that he controls the course of events in the universe – a belief in which Muslims and Christians are more or less in agreement. The Bible and the Qur'ān are both accepted as the word or speech of God, though Muslims and Christians may differ a little in their understanding of this. Also included among the doctrines to be accepted because of this verification must be the Islamic doctrine of the prophethood of Muḥammad and the Christian doctrine of the incarnation of Jesus. Superficially neither of these is acceptable to the other religion but, when the doctrines are looked at more closely, the reader will probably find that the divergences are less than they appeared at first sight.

II A justification of the linguistic form of religious truth

Religious truth is frequently criticized and rejected because it employs metaphorical expressions, figures of speech, poetic images and mythic or mythological conceptions. This criticism is based on mistaken ideas about the relation of language to reality, but in order to refute it the matter requires to be looked at in some detail.

(a) Symbolic language as an expression of reality

In this book the terms 'symbol' and 'symbolic language' are used in a very wide sense to cover whatever is not 'primary language'. The word 'symbol' has been preferred because it is mostly used with a positive connotation. For some senses the words 'metaphor' and 'myth' are alternatives, but both these often have the negative connotation of 'unreality' in the thought of ordinary people, even if some theologians, especially in America, use 'myth' in a positive sense.[14] In a recent book Hans Küng speaks of 'the metaphorical language of images'.[15]

By 'primary language' here is to be understood the common words of ordinary life for bodies, qualities, actions, relations and the like; e.g. table, house, river, blue, sweet, quick, walk, sing, over, after, son, cousin, king, slave. In most languages these words are either the primary, basic roots or are closely associated with them. They indicate the patterns found in experience at a fairly simple level.[16] Many of the patterns can be indicated by pointing. Others, such as the relationships within a family are learnt in the course of social life. A child probably knows the social meaning of 'son' and 'cousin' long before he knows about the acts which are the basis of these relationships.

By 'symbolic language' is here being understood whatever is not primary. When a symbolic name is given to a novel object it is normally based on some resemblance to an object with a primary name; the bulb of the electric variety is doubtless so called because in shape it resembles the bulb in the garden. The fact that the name is symbolic or metaphorical in origin does not make any difficulties in practice after we have had a little experience of electric bulbs; we know that we do not acquire new bulbs by planting one in the garden.

When we come to abstract conceptions and complex patterns, there is no escape from symbolic language. Most of the terms used in discussing intellectual questions are symbolic, such as: 'the *influence* of Darwin', 'the existentialist *movement* in philosophy', 'political *revolutions*', '*unbridled* individualism'. The propriety in general of using such terms is not questioned. Even when we question a particular assertion, we accept the terms used in making the assertion. With the commoner terms we are often unaware of their symbolic character. When we speak of the French Revolution, we do not think of a wheel revolving, and indeed the word 'revolution' in its political use has acquired connotations which are derived from experience of politics rather than from observation of wheels. In these cases, then, the symbolic or metaphorical terms are used to indicate patterns which are really found in the material, and the only doubt about them is due to the possibility that there may be alternative patterns in the same material and that these alternative patterns may be more appropriate for our purposes.

Some modern scientists try to avoid metaphor wherever possible. In the argument whether light is to be thought of as 'waves' or 'particles' it would be claimed that these metaphors are used in order to make things clearer to the layman. The historians of science, however, have no such hesitations. A popular book in this field was called 'The *architecture* of matter',[17] and had headings such as 'the new *climate* of thought', 'the scientific *legacy* of the Stoics', 'the *empire* of classical physics' and '*entering* the quantum *world*'. Biologists, too, appear to be happy with such terms as 'natural *selection*' and 'epigenetic *slope*'. The point need not be further laboured that the way in which a pattern is named does not affect the reality of the pattern. For a time some scientists would not accept Darwin's theory of natural selection, but this was because they had no evidence that the pattern existed in the facts, not because they objected to the use of a metaphor.

An adequate discussion of the use of metaphor in poetry is beyond our present scope.[18] It may be noted, however, that poetical metaphors call attention to patterns in our field of awareness, and to this extent are pattern-symbols. When Wordsworth speaks of daffodils 'fluttering and dancing in the breeze', he sees in the wind-swept daffodils a pattern resembling that of birds or insects fluttering and people dancing, and by this language calls the reader's attention to this pattern. Why we find poetical metaphors pleasing is, of course, another question.

Conventional symbols are those where there is no resemblance between the symbol and the thing symbolized, but only a relationship based on convention. Thus a flag symbolizes a country, a shape such as a cross or the star of David symbolizes a religion or religious community, a diagram of a wheel-chair symbolizes disabled persons or some facility for them. and so on. Words, apart from onomatopoeia, are conventional symbols; so also are initials and trade-marks. Analogously to pattern-symbols, the fact that conventional symbols have originated in a certain way does not affect the reality of what they symbolize, though its reality may be affected in other ways; e.g. it may have ceased to exist or may never have existed (as some would claim of a UFO). Where the conventional symbol is a material object, such as a flag or a crucifix, it may come to be identified in men's minds with the thing symbolized, in such a way that the devotion felt towards the country or the divine person comes to be directed towards the symbol. Such transference, however, is not restricted to instances where there is something like a religious element. The photograph of a loved person or place may evoke happy memories and appropriate feelings. The transference of feelings from thing symbolized to the symbol is thus a psychological phenomenon to be noted, but does not affect the relation of the symbol to the reality symbolized.

The third type of symbols are the elemental symbols. The term is taken from Ira Progoff, who describes them as follows:

> The Elemental Symbols are reflections in man of the primary processes of the universe in their varied phases and aspects. The infinity of the universe encompasses man. It excites his wonder, but it eludes his knowledge. Nonetheless, some quality of its infinity seems to be part of the nature of the human being. It is present in him as the equivalent in human form of the creative principle that pervades the universe. It expresses the kinship of man to the rest of creation. The psyche with its reflecting faculty acts as a mirror for

> the principles by which the infinity of the universe disperses itself and becomes finite in particular forms and patterns.[19]

In this passage the reference is ultimately to the field of religion, though overt religious terminology is carefully avoided. The elemental symbols appear to be roughly what Jung meant by 'archetypes', and for which I have elsewhere employed the phrase 'the dynamic or archetypal element' in religious ideation.[20]

The elemental symbols may also be approached from the standpoint of a definition of religion put forward (for limited purposes) by R. N. Bellah in 1964. According to this definition religion is 'a set of symbolic forms and acts which relate man to the ultimate conditions of his existence'.[21] Religious symbolization thus relates man to the higher, supernatural or divine powers on which his life is dependent, but it 'is also involved in relating him to himself and in symbolizing his own identity'.[22] Our relation to higher powers is often expressed by a dynamic or archetypal idea which is derived from family relationships. The idea of the mother is universally of great importance, both in early religions as the Earth Mother or Great Mother, particularized as Cybele, Demeter, Ashtoreth (Ishtar, Astarte) or Isis, and in Christianity as the Blessed Virgin Mary (the 'virgin mother') and Mother Church. Fatherhood is seen in the first hypostasis of the Christian Trinity and also in the 'father of gods and men' of Greek mythology. Sonship is associated with the second hypostasis of the Trinity, but also comes to be merged with the ideas of the inspired leader, the anointed king and the like.

In many cases these dynamic ideas appear to arise within human beings and then, as it were, to go about looking for some appropriate person to become the 'bearer' of the 'projection'. Shī'ite Muslims, for example, seem to have found it necessary that there should be an imam or infallible leader, and to have selected 'Alī and his descendants to be 'bearers' of the idea. Opponents felt that these persons were inappropriate as imams, but this did not lessen the Shī'ites' devotion to them. In the Old Testament about 520 BC, when life in Jerusalem was proving difficult for the returned exiles and many were hoping for a messiah or inspired leader, even the prophets Haggai (2.20-3) and Zechariah (4.6-10) attached the messianic image to Zerubbabel, the high commissioner; but in the end, though much was accomplished and the building of the Second Temple begun, Zerubbabel somehow did not come up to their expectations and no more is heard of him.[23] It further appears that, when the dynamic image of the leader becomes attached to a particular man, great devotion towards him wells up in the hearts of his followers, at least so long as they believe in his worthiness to bear the image.

The dynamic images are not restricted to those mentioned. Almost any natural object or natural process may be used as a symbol. In many religions the annual death and revival of vegetation symbolized human death and resurrection. Among other symbols are to be found birds, eggs, trees, water, mountains, caves, burial, the moon, and so on.[24] Progoff describes a case in which open spaces within the structure of a stone became an important symbol for a man. Because so many objects and processes can become symbols, it is plausible to think that these elemental symbols are functioning in somewhat the same way as the pattern-symbols of the first type. They help us to become aware of complex patterns in those aspects of our experience in which there is present something of our relationship to the ultimate conditions of our existence. There is a difference, however, between the elemental symbols and the usual pattern-symbols. In the case of the latter we have a clear idea or perception of the thing symbolized, whether it be the French Revolution or an electric bulb. The elemental symbols, on the other hand, refer to patterns in a field of which we have only a dim and unclear awareness, and where we sometimes have to search arduously in order to find the patterns (especially when they are patterns suggested to us by external religious authority—'have you experienced rebirth?' for example). Symbols which arise spontaneously within oneself, as in the case described by Progoff, are perhaps more easily traced within one's experience, but they seldom have the wide validity of the great religious symbols.

Because the elemental symbols help us to become aware of certain patterns in our experience and so to conceptualize it, and because of their greater clarity, we tend to hold the symbols before our minds rather than the unclear experience in which the patterns are embedded. In this way the symbol becomes identified with the symbolized. Unless we are unduly naïve. however, there is little danger of confusion here. It is commonly found that the meaning of a symbol cannot be fully comprehended in intellectual formulations, there are always further depths not yet expressed, and perhaps in part unknown; but what controls the formulations is not the clear idea of the symbol but the unclear experience.

From this brief survey of different kinds of symbols and symbolic language it is clear that the use of a symbolic or metaphorical term does not imply the unreality of what the term denotes. The electric bulb is not a botanical bulb, but it is still a completely real object. Moreover, our knowledge of electric bulbs owes nothing to botany but comes entirely from our experience of dealing with electric bulbs. Similarly, what scientists know about atoms is derived from countless experiments, mostly during the last two centuries, and owes nothing to the fact that an 'atom' was originally an 'uncuttable' portion of matter. In both cases the symbolic or metaphorical origin of the term is irrelevant to its present-day use.

With regard to terms like 'influence', 'movement' and 'revolution' the matter is slightly different. These roughly indicate complex patterns embedded in a great mass of facts; but the question at issue is not so much whether the pattern is really there (since it usually is), as whether it is important and significant for our understanding of what happened. There is undoubtedly a great mass of phenomena to which the term 'French Revolution' is commonly applied, and this has proved convenient; but it is not nonsensical to ask whether this is the best way of describing the phenomena or whether some alternative pattern might have advantages. Yet even if the pattern indicated by the symbolic term is not important, it at least exists.

(b) Symbolic language in religious matters

The fact that in non-religious matters symbolic language does not imply unreality suggests that the same should be true in religious assertions. Just as the secular historian finds patterns in a great mass of events, so the assertion that 'God controls the course of history' indicates a pattern embedded in a great mass of material. This material includes not merely the history found in the Bible and the Qur'ān but also the later historical experiences of the Jewish, Christian and Islamic communities and of individual members of these communities. For these communities the broad lines of their scriptural history are part of their dogmatic basis. In the case of later events, however, there is nearly always the possibility of alternative patterns. Thus if something good happens to an individual, he may say, 'Did God do this for me, or was it just a lucky chance?' In personal matters or events of recent political history it may be difficult to answer such a question; but the witness of the three religious communities over centuries is that the course of history is under God's control, even if one cannot show in every case what his purposes are.

Again the fact that God commands us to act in certain ways has a scriptural basis, but is also supported by various forms of inner experience, such as the internalization of social norms (the feeling that one ought or ought not to do acts of certain types) and the inner promptings which come to individuals to perform particular acts. Temporal rewards and punishments from God are part of the pattern of his control of history, as is also his strengthening of men to gain victory in battle, and his achievement of his purposes through prophets, saints and other outstanding men and women. In this way most of the dogmas about God's activity within the historical process may be described as patterns based on a mass of material found in communal experience. Problems of detail and problems raised by assertions which go beyond the historical process will be dealt with in succeeding chapters.

From early times believers in God have been aware of the incompleteness of their knowledge of God. In the Bible this is discussed in terms of whether man can 'see' God (which, of course, is symbolic language); but there are discrepant statements. Where the New Testament states categorically that 'no man has seen God at any time',[25] the Old Testament appears to allow a limited vision or seeing of God. At Sinai Moses, though not shown God's face, was shown his 'back parts'; at the same time, however, it is emphasized that any fuller awareness of God is dangerous and destructive for man – 'for there shall no man see me and live'.[26] Despite this passage Isaiah and Job speak of themselves as having seen God, though there is a hint that the experience came near to being destructive. Isaiah describes how in the year of King Uzziah's death he saw God seated on a throne, high and lifted up, with worshipping seraphim round about him; and then he exclaims, 'Woe is me! for I am undone, because I am a man of unclean lips . . . for mine eyes have seen the King, the Lord of hosts.'[27] Isaiah is reassured, however, when a seraph touches his lips with a live coal from the altar and tells him that his sin has been taken away. Then he hears God's voice and received an 'inner prompting' to his prophetic vocation. Job, after his long arguments with his friends and with God, is finally somehow aware of God's glory and majesty – 'I have heard of you by the hearing of the ear, but now my eye sees you'; and his reaction to the experience is that 'I abhor myself and repent in dust and ashes.'[28] In heaven, on the other hand, Paul looks forward to knowing God 'even as also he is known'.[29]

The Qur'ān apparently denies that God can be seen by men in this life—'the eyes do not apprehend him, but he apprehends the eyes' (6.103); but Muslim scholars mostly hold that God will be seen in Heaven by the believers, basing their view on the verse, 'faces on that day are bright, looking to their Lord' (75.22f.).

The ground for the application of human terms to God is some resemblance of pattern. If he is spoken of as 'father', either of the believers or of all men, this is because there is something fatherlike in his relation to them. This 'something' could perhaps be expressed by saying that he was 'caring', but, apart from the fact that this is also symbolic, many people would hold that it is far from bringing out the full significance of the term 'father'. Especially in the case of archetypal symbols applied to God there always seems to be some residue of meaning which is not conveyed by any 'translations' or circumlocutions. Since these deal with our relationship to the ultimate conditions of our existence, they tend to refer to patterns of great complexity in our experience, where we have only a dim, unclear and incomplete awareness of what is symbolized. Sometimes we have to search arduously in our experience for the patterns of which a religious tradition speaks. In general, then, in religious matters it is found that symbolic language is not fully descriptive but rather suggestive or evocative. That is to say, it hints at or suggests complex but unclear patterns where there is perhaps also some fluidity; and even at best the account it gives is incomplete, since the reality is more than the symbolic pattern.

It is instructive to notice how Muslim scholars dealt with the anthropomorphic terms in the Qur'ān. Some held they were metaphors, and tried to find comparable metaphorical usages in non-religious contexts. They would find an Arabic phrase similar to the English 'Give me a hand', meaning 'help', and would then argue that 'the hand of God' meant the 'help' he gives. Other scholars, while agreeing that God could not have a physical or bodily hand (that is, not a hand in the literal sense), felt there was some loss of meaning in the non-metaphorical 'translation' of the term. They therefore maintained that the anthropomorphic terms applied to God were to be understood *bi-lā kayf*, 'without (specifying) how' or 'amodally', that is, without asking whether they were literal or metaphorical. This is an entirely rational approach to the problem, and one of great subtlety. If the terms are treated as metaphors (used in a secondary sense) and translated into non-metaphorical language, there is a danger that much will be lost. It is thus better to accept the terms as they stand and deliberately to refrain from asking epistemological questions. The attitude might be called one of 'sophisticated naivety'. A Christian thinker of the seventeenth century offers an interesting parallel to the Arabic phrase; Joseph Glanvill argued that reason supports religion by showing, among other things, that we 'must not expect thoroughly to understand the deeper things of God; . . . and that 'tis the highest reason in the world to believe that what he saith is true, though we do not know how these things are'.[30]

Many Christians, I believe, show this sophisticated naivety when they engage in prayer. They know that they are not literally speaking to God as they would to another human being, and that he does not literally hear them; but they believe that through this symbolic action they are in touch with something of ultimate reality, and that because of it God effects something for them and for the world.

Two further points may be made. Firstly, because of the evocative and non-descriptive character of symbolic language, it cannot be adequately replaced by any 'translation' into non-symbolic or less obviously symbolic language. Symbolic language is indeed often the best way and sometimes the only way of expressing certain aspects of ultimate reality. Secondly, though the knowledge of God attained by symbolic language is incomplete, it is sufficient for our guidance in the practical business of living. Intellectually it may disappoint hopes and expectations, but practically it makes it possible for us to 'relate ourselves to the ultimate conditions of our existence' in a way that is wholly satisfactory.

III Critique of the assumptions of scientism

While it is taken as axiomatic in this book that the assured results of science are to be accepted, these assured results have to be carefully distinguished from a body of assumptions sometimes called 'scientism'. These assumptions are closely associated with science and are thought by some to be proved by it, but they are in fact unproved assumptions belonging more to the sphere of philosophy than to that of science. Three points will be specially considered here: (1) that the objects studied by the sciences are the sole reality; (2) that the account of the original form of a thing shows what it really is; and (3) that analysis of a thing into parts shows what it really is. Since these assumptions contradict in certain ways the common-sense view of reality, it is important to begin by noting the fundamental character of this last.

(a) The fundamental character of the common-sense view of reality

By the common-sense view of reality is meant the view held by the ordinary man before he has engaged in any philosophical reflection or extensive scientific activity or theological study. It is the ordinary man of the Western world who is in question here, and the possibility must be left open that there are slight differences in the common-sense views of men of other cultures. It may also be allowed that some elementary results of science are now included in the common-sense view.

The elements in the common-sense view with which we shall be chiefly concerned are the following: man has to act in a world in which there are material bodies and other human beings, and his actions have to take account of these and also have effects upon them; events and actions each occur at a particular location in space and at a particular moment in time; the agent has some knowledge of himself and of his freedom in acting; actions and events normally include a social meaning, that is, a relation to a complex network of human activities. Since all that has been mentioned here is accepted as real it is comprised in the common-sense view of reality. In previous ages the main social norms were also included in this common-sense view, but at the present time in parts of the Western world very little of this has been left.

It must be emphasized once more that this common-sense view of reality, whose basic elements have just been listed, has been massively verified over countless millennia. All sane and reasonable human beings make this common-sense view the basis of all their actions, and indeed cannot do otherwise. Even Descartes, engaging in his intellectual experiment, could not but continue his daily life on the basis of the common-sense view. The experiential verification of the common-sense view is, of course, subject to certain qualifications. All that is claimed for it is that it is true in those respects which are relevant to its practical successes. Philosophical reflection has shown that it is in need of correction in some respects, or at least of what may be called refinement. To use an old example – the shadow of the gnomon of a sundial appears to be stationary; but if one looks at it an hour later, one finds that it has in fact moved, and further observation shows that it has not moved by jumps but must have been moving slowly all the time.[31] Among the reasons Descartes gives for rejecting all ordinary knowledge except the *Cogito* are cases where the senses mislead us, the similarity of dreams and waking life, and erroneous argumentation.[32]

In so far as the common-sense view of reality is the view held by men before they undertake philosophical reflection or scientific research, it is almost tautologous to say that this is the basis of their philosophy and their science. It is, of course, true that the philosopher and the scientist must continue to base their daily lives on the common-sense view. More important, however, is the fact that even in their philosophical and scientific work they continue to assume the reliability in a general way of the common-sense view. The proof of the deceptiveness of the senses from the shadow of the gnomon presupposes the accuracy of the first observation of the shadow and also of the second observation an hour later, and indeed of a third observation prolonged over at least part of an hour in order to ensure that there are no jumps. In most sciences the correctness is presupposed of many observations at the common-sense level, from the common-sense properties of chemical substances to the shapes and colours of parts of animals and plants; readings of scientific instruments are also made at the common-sense level.

Since philosophy and science thus presuppose the general reliability of the common-sense view of reality, while allowing that it may be mistaken in a relatively small number of points, it follows that Descartes was mistaken in thinking that *cogito ergo sum* is our only certainty. The proper course for both the philosopher and the scientist is to consider how any palpable errors in the common-sense view may be corrected and any naive elements refined and given greater subtlety.

By way of illustration we may consider the philosophical treatment of the common-sense view of 'seeing a table'. The philosopher notes that the table appears differently to the viewer from different angles, but none of the appearances can be identified with the table. It is always seen from a particular perspective, never 'as it is in itself' (as is sometimes said). We can, of course, form a concept of the table 'as it is in itself'; this concept would be not unlike the plans used by the workman making the table, and might have something such as front elevation, side elevation, ground level, table-top level. The appearances and the concept are still not the whole of our experience with tables. We have also acquired skills to make the necessary adjustments to perspective when dealing with tables practically, whether setting them for meals or writing on them or moving them about. Most philosophers are aware of this complexity in our apprehension of a table, and describe and explain it in various ways, some of which have been mentioned above. The details, however, may be passed over since they are not directly relevant to the present discussion.

The statements of the philosophers that, when we see a table, we see it as 'a family of sense-data' or 'an ordered series of its manifestations', though ostensibly about the table are more about the process of seeing it; and the common-sense view of the table is to be distinguished from the common-sense view of what happens when one sees it. The ordinary person tends to suppose that he looks in a certain direction and sees a table; and that is all there is to it. He enters a room, where he has never been before, and within a few seconds says, 'That is a fine table—Chippendale, I think.' Although the awareness and assessment of the table seem to happen instantaneously, he must have unconsciously compared the object in the room with his general experience of tables and also, perhaps half consciously, with his experience of the class of Chippendale tables and of other similar but distinct classes of antique tables.

Since the common-sense view of seeing a table 'works' in practice, at least up to a point, it must be true in certain respects. The most important points are that the sense of sight (or visual perception) is in general reliable and that it provides a direct and immediate relation (in some sense) between the viewer and the object seen. This 'immediacy' ignores, but does not deny, the presence of light-waves, which one takes to be unknown to common sense; but the ordinary person realizes that he cannot see in the absence of light, and, if he wants to see in the dark, takes steps to make light. In the course of his life, too, the ordinary person becomes aware of the situations where sight is not entirely reliable. If he collects mushrooms from nearby fields, he knows that at a distance he cannot infallibly distinguish a mushroom from a piece of paper or a white stone, and that he must go nearer in order to be sure that the white patch is not a piece of paper. If he sketches, he develops some idea of the rules of perspective. In general, then, he knows that he is able to rely on sight and that, if he turns his eyes in a given direction, he will see whatever there is to be seen.

Between this common-sense view and philosophical views there is no ultimate contradiction, even though some philosophers have suggested that their theories should replace the common-sense view. A philosophical view is a refinement rather than a correction of the common-sense view. It shows the complexity of what the ordinary man takes to be simple, and so is justified, indeed necessary, in philosophical activity. For most practical purposes of daily life, however, the common-sense view is more adequate because of its greater simplicity; that is, it enables people to know more adequately the reality with which they have to deal in their actions.

(b) Reality and the objects studied by science

The first assumption to be considered, namely, that the objects studied by the sciences are the sole reality, is sometimes given the more extreme formulation that only the physical or physico-chemical event is the real event. This, in some form or other, is believed by many scientists. Michael Polanyi goes so far as to say that 'the ideal of science remains what it was in the time of Laplace: to replace all human knowledge by a knowledge of atoms in motion'.[33] From this assumption, if it is taken as true, it is possible to infer that there is no such thing as human mind or consciousness and no such thing as human freedom and responsibility; the phenomena leading to belief in mind and freedom are said to be adequately explained by purely physical events such as the movement of atoms. Not all scientists would subscribe to these last two inferences, but some scientists and others suppose that science has proved them.

If the universe is thought of as process, then events are more fundamental than bodies, but for the purpose of the exposition here it will be simpler to deal with bodies. Let us then begin by considering the common-sense view of a table. According to this the table is a material body of a particular shape. The chief element in this shape is a steady flat surface, usually two or three feet from the ground, on which one may lay other material objects like plates, books or machines. There are also legs or something similar to keep the flat surface at this height. Since the table is a human artefact, the extent and height of the table-top will depend on the precise purpose for which it is intended. The table is made of wood, steel or some other rigid material. For the scientist, on the other hand, the shape of the table will be specified by a number of plans or sets of co-ordinates. If the table is of steel, he will state the precise chemical composition of the steel alloy employed, and will give a general account of the molecules, atoms and subatomic particles involved.

The question at issue is whether the table as described by science is the *real* table in some sense which makes the common-sense table less real. The position to be adopted here is that both the scientific account and the common-sense account of the table are true, but that the scientific account is relevant only in the context of certain scientific activities, whereas the common-sense account is relevant in the context of ordinary life. As already noted, the scientific account is so complex that it would hinder rather than help the housewife in the business of setting the table for a meal. The common-sense conception of the table, on the other hand, is greatly simplified, and normally contains only what is necessary for efficiency in action.

The scientific account also omits an essential element in the conception of the table, namely, its human meaning, that is, the fact that it is for laying things on. The importance of this meaning is not so clear in the case of the table, but it becomes obvious if we consider Alan and the Blues playing a game of football and winning the cup. It is conceivable that by the use of several cameras the game could be fully recorded and that all the movements of the ball and of the players could then be expressed mathematically. Yet this would not tell anyone how the game really went. The movement of the ball passing between the goal posts is not very different physically from any other part of its movement. To explain the significance of passing between the posts there would have to be a scientific account of the vast social network of which this is a part. Michael Polanyi has remarked that 'most biologists would declare that both the principles of structure and of organizing fields will be reduced one day to the laws of physics and chemistry'; and some scientists might be inclined to make a similar statement about social matters. Polanyi continues, however, 'but I am unable to discover the grounds—or even understand the meaning—of such assurances . . .';[34] and this would apply even more forcibly in the social field. So far as the present discussion is concerned, the point might be made that, even if *per impossibile* all social life came to be described in physico-chemical terms, the description would be so complex that men would have to translate it back into simpler terms before they could understand it or act on it; and these terms would be similar to those of common sense. The event described as 'Alan kicked the goal which won the cup for the Blues' certainly has a physico-chemical component or infrastructure, which is coterminous with the event. Yet the real event is not the prodigiously complex physico-chemical process but simply Alan kicking the goal which won the match.

The conclusion up to this point, then, is that meanings are just as real as molecules, since they are part of the reality in response to which we act. A failure, when acting, to take account of the relevant human and social meanings is just as disastrous as stepping out of a sixty-foot-high window or eating a poisonous mushroom. This conclusion further implies that reality is more extensive than the objects of scientific study, at least than those of physics and other natural sciences. In this way it invalidates an argument against the existence of 'spiritual beings' (such as God and angels). It cannot be said that these are impossible because they are not objects of scientific study; and it is thus left open to believers in them to assert their existence on other grounds.

(c) Reality and origins

The second assumption to be considered is that the original form of a thing shows what it really is. The reductionist attempt to explain things by tracing them to their origins has had some successes. To think of early men and of ourselves their descendants as naked apes, without fur to protect them from cold, gives insight into certain aspects of human development. Similarly, we get some insight into the motivations underlying a philosopher's thinking by looking at his psychological and socio-political background, that is, the circumstances of his childhood.[35] Despite the insight gained, however, this study of origins does not show us what the things *really* are. A human being is not really just a naked ape any more than he is just an overgrown amoeba; he has outgrown these stages. The philosophy of a great thinker is not just the intellectual outpourings of a neurotic child, but has to be judged by the philosophical quality of his mature publications and not by his infantile tendencies.

The error of trying to assess things by their origins is very clear when one looks at the highest achievements of humanity in science, philosophy, art, music, literature and religion. The individuals who achieved these things always had a psychosomatic constitution and a socio-political background; but these factors, though in one sense essential, are not the basis of our judgments of the finished products. Shakespeare had a source for the story of *Hamlet* and did not invent it, but his play is judged by its own qualitites as a play, and we admire the creative genius which could so transform the source. There are peculiarities and idiosyncrasies in the psychological make-up of Descartes, Kant, Goethe and many other thinkers and writers, and this may help us to understand how they came to write as they did; but the books must ultimately be judged by the quality of the thought expressed in them, and by the influence of that thought on contemporaries and successors. Somewhat similar is the relation of our species today to its prehuman or early human ancestors. It is probably the case that for many generations these were aggressive killers, and could not have survived had they not been so. That does not mean, however, that we, their descendants, must inevitably go on being aggressive killers. This is no more inevitable for us than is the habit of eating meat raw; and indeed in present circumstances the overcoming or sublimation of this ancestral trait of aggressiveness has become a condition of mankind's survival.

Something like this principle is found in Karl Rahner's discussion of non-Christian religions.[36] He allows that they have both a natural and a supernatural knowledge of God, and sees them as forms of 'anonymous Christianity'. For members of *any* religion this is an important way of considering other religions. They may be regarded as immature forms of the one world-religion of the future, whatever that is to be. Rahner holds that it will be Christianity; but it might be more realistic to look upon Christianity as still in some respects immature, even if one also held that the one world-religion of the future would be in some sense continuous with it. It is also important to remember, however, that progress to maturity is not automatic, and that neither organisms nor communities go on all the time developing into something better. The Qur'ān regards Judaism and Christianity as having deviated from their pristine purity of doctrine; and many observers today would assert that there are instances where a religion, without changing its formal doctrine, had somehow deteriorated and become a vehicle of unwholesome attitudes—including what Marx meant by an 'opiate for the masses'.

The question of the relation of the mature to the immature also comes up in connection with the interpretation of scripture. Many scholars hold that the author of the Fourth Gospel was presenting a picture of Jesus as he had come to see him with hindsight and after much reflection. The above discussion of origins would suggest that the Fourth Gospel may be accepted as true in the sense that the writer is bringing out patterns that were already inherent in the events but not yet explicit. On the other hand, the traditional Christian interpretation (Matthew 1.23) of the words 'a virgin shall conceive' (Isaiah 7.14) as foretelling the birth of Jesus is not altogether justified, since according to the scholars the word translated 'virgin' merely means 'young woman' without specifying virginity or the opposite, and the whole passage is primarily concerned to indicate a period of a few years. Something similar may be true of the Qur'ānic phrase *khāṭam an-nabiyyīn*, 'the seal of the prophets' (33.40), which modern Muslims unanimously interpret as the last of the prophets after whom there will be no others, whereas it is probable that for the first hearers the meaning was that he was the seal confirming previous prophets.

(d) Reality and analysis into parts

The third assumption is that the analysis of a thing into parts shows what it really is. This method of analysing something into simpler constituent parts is of proven worth in science, notably in chemistry. It has shown its ability to achieve important results, and has become the basis of much scientific and science-based technological activity. Yet even where the method of analysis is successful, it is difficult to say precisely what it tells us about reality. Common salt shows on analysis that it consists of sodium and chlorine, though these are not simply mixed with one another but are chemically combined. Now this fact about salt, and countless other similar facts discovered by chemistry, are of great importance for various kinds of scientific activity (which may ultimately benefit the ordinary man), but are irrelevant to most uses of salt and other substances in daily life. The chemical formula for salt does not even begin to tie up with our ordinary everyday experience of salt—its taste, its preservative qualities and the like. Indeed, it becomes mysterious that something with the properties of salt should be produced by the chemical combination of sodium and chlorine. In other words, chemical analysis leads to knowledge of useful facts about salt, but does not change our experiential knowledge of what salt really is, that is, the knowledge on which we base decisions involving salt in the course of our everyday living.

What has just been said leads up to the difficult question of whether chemistry can be reduced to physics, but this may be left aside here in favour of the more serious and more difficult question of the relationship of living things, and human beings in particular, to the physico-chemical basis of their life. Are we just physico-chemical structures, or is there something more to us? In this somewhat technical matter it seems best not to attempt an independent discussion, but to rely on the expertise of Michael Polanyi and give a summary of his argument as it is found in one of his latest articles.[37]

Polanyi begins his exposition by emphasizing a fact about machines.

> The machine as a whole works under the control of two distinct principles. The higher one is the principle of the machine's design, and this harnesses the lower one, which consists in the physical

> chemical processes on which the machine relies.[38]

The higher principle may then be said to impose boundary conditions or a boundary on the laws of physics and chemistry. Something similar is observed in the machine-like functioning of the organs of animals. From this he goes on to assert the existence of a hierarchy of principles in human beings.

> The theory of boundary conditions recognized the higher levels of life as forming a hierarchy, each level of which relies for its workings on the principles of the levels below it, even while it itself is irreducible to these lower principles.[39]

He then gives an indication of what these principles are:

> The lowest functions of life are those called vegetative; these vegetative functions, sustaining life at its lowest level, leave open —both in plants and in animals—the higher functions of growth and in animals also leave open the operations of muscular actions; next in turn, the principles governing muscular actions in animals leave open the integration of such actions to innate patterns of behaviour; and, again, such patterns are open in their turn to be shaped by intelligence, while the working of intelligence itself can be made to serve in man the still higher principles of a responsible choice.[40]

The final conclusion, to which we shall return later, is that though rooted in the body, the mind is free in its actions—exactly as our common sense knows it to be free.[41]

The hierarchy of principles in man can be illustrated by the parallel case of verbal communication, for example, in a speech by a distinguished orator. The lowest level here is the production of sounds. These are controlled by vocabulary, but do not control it. The next level is that of grammar, which controls the form of words. Above grammar comes style, Finally comes the content of the speech, which controls the lower levels, but is not itself controlled by vocabulary, grammar or even style.

Polanyi's conception of a hierarchy of principles gives insight into the reality of an event such as Alan's kicking of the winning goal in the cup final. Analysis, whether physical, chemical or physiological, does not show the reality of the event. It can only be known in its reality in the context of the dove-tailing 'responsible choices' of vast numbers of human beings.

It is not always the case, of course, that the higher principles maintain control of the lower. Chemical deficiencies, for example, may impair the functioning of higher-level principles in man. In general, it appears that lower-level processes in a human being are able to evade higher control. In the extreme case this leads to death. Cases such as this, however, do not invalidate the rule that in normal functioning the higher controls the lower.

The method of analysis, as just described, is not restricted to science, but has a distinguished history in philosophy. John Locke's 'simple ideas of sensation' and the 'sense-data' of recent British empiricists are simple constituents from which more complex ideas or percepts may be built up. Such philosophical analysis is open to criticisms comparable to those made of scientific analysis. An alternative method was first developed by the Gestalt psychologists, and has attracted the attention of some philosophers. Some elementary considerations about this method will be in place here.

The English word 'pattern' seems adequate to represent 'Gestalt'. By 'pattern' I understand a multiplicity regarded as a whole, and such that the whole has qualities different from and additional to those of the parts composing it. A simple example of a pattern would be a painting. This is composed of patches of colour, but even a modern abstract painting is something more than a collecton of patches of colour. Moreover, one is often aware of the painting as a whole before one is aware of the details. If one first sees the painting at the end of a long gallery, only a general impression of it is possible; but as one moves nearer, one is able to distinguish more and more details. In general, then, awareness of a pattern as a whole may precede in time awareness of the details or items of which it is composed. This apprehension of the pattern before the details happens very frequently in daily life. We see a man, a tree, a book, an egg, a rose, a banana, a house, a river, and so on. For present purposes all these are patterns, since they are multiplicities which we regard as wholes.

A further point to note is that different patterns may be found in the same complex object. Thus a chess-board may be regarded as consisting of sixty-four squares alternately black and white. It may also be regarded, however, as consisting of sixteen squares, of which each consists of four of the smaller squares arranged alternately; or of sixteen pieces, of which each consists of four smaller squares in a row; or of sixteen L-shaped pieces of four smaller squares, where three make the long leg of the L; or one of numerous other possibilities.

The existence of alternative patterns in the same material is sometimes of theoretical importance. Even in the history of science the chemical theory of phlogiston, which was popular for a time, seems to have been based on patterns which genuinely existed in the material produced by chemical experiment; and the abandonment of the theory was due partly to the discovery of other material in which the patterns did not occur and partly to the failure of the theory to provide adequate causal explanations of various phenomena. In the material studied by general historians there are normally many alternative patterns to be discovered; and the historian selects for emphasis those patterns which are relevant to his own interests and those of his readers. Thus Arnold Toynbee based his *Study of History* on the discovery that certain patterns were repeated in the different areas of history which he called civilizations; but towards the end of his life he realized that he could have selected different patterns–he could, for example, have given central place to 'universal religions'–and that he then might have reached significantly different results.

Perhaps the point at which the existence of alternative patterns is most important is in respect of the categorial differences between cultures or civilizations.[42] At some primitive period people in a certain region of the earth discovered certain patterns in the world around them, and made use of these patterns in working out a general world-view. In other regions other people used slightly different patterns. In the course of time the great world-religions worked out their world-views in terms of different categories of fundamental patterns; and this makes communication and 'dialogue' between them a matter of great difficulty. Until the development of transoceanic navigation by the Europeans in the fifteenth century the great religions existed in relative isolation from one another, each in its own distinctive cultural area. Contemporary interreligious problems are mainly due to improved communications. It is difficult to give precise formulations of the categorial differences.[43] It will perhaps suffice here to call attention to a categorial difference which has developed among ourselves during the twentieth century. This is the difference between thinking of reality as consisting of substances which endure through time and thinking of reality as consisting of events which are grouped together to form the spatio-temporal process.

The discussion of this third assumption points to the conclusion that to analyse a thing into its parts, though sometimes useful and important, does not show what the thing really is, since there are wholes which are more than the sum of their parts, and even wholes in which a central or holistic factor somehow controls the parts. This last point will reappear in a later chapter.

Chapter 3

The names and attributes of God

Both Islam and Christianity assert the existence of God, and do so kerygmatically. That is to say, it is not asserted provisionally like a scientific hypothesis, but is made as an affirmative statement or even a joyful proclamation about reality. Moreover, if a person accepts it, it affects his life, since he has to commit himself to this view of reality and base his conduct on it. While most of the rest of the book will be dealing with various aspects of belief in God, the purpose of the present chapter is to look at certain general matters. Later chapters will consider more specific points: God revealing himself through scriptures, God as creator and sustainer of the universe, God as the Lord of history, and God in relation to human beings.

I The general agreement of Islam and Christianity about God

Muslims and Christians who discuss religious questions with one another quickly discover that they have to accept one another as fellow-believers in God. Thus a mixed group of Muslim and Christian scholars produced a book, first in German, then in English, entitled *We Believe in One God: The experience of God in Christianity and Islam.*[1] There are some Christians and also Muslims, however, who would deny that the two religions worship the same God; and so some further consideration must be given to the point.

Islam originated in a region of the world which already had some knowledge of God through Judaism, Christianity and Zoroastrianism. In Arabia and the surrounding lands there was also widespread a form of the old Semitic religion in which people who worshipped pagan deities also acknowledged a 'high god' superior to these. Several verses of the Qur'ān are evidence for the existence at Mecca of persons who, in addition to other gods, acknowledged Allāh as a 'high god'.[2] The name *Allāh* was thus familiar to the people of Mecca before Muḥammad, and was accepted into Islam together with the insistence that 'there is no deity but *Allāh*, God'. The Qur'ān regards Islam as parallel to other religions, including Judaism and Christianity, and as identical with the religion of Abraham. Moses and Jesus, the founders of Judaism and Christianity, are further regarded as having proclaimed the same truths as Abraham, but there is no idea of a prophetic tradition, since each is held to have received the message directly from God. While the Qur'ān also speaks of the Jews and Christians as having deviated from the pure religion of Abraham in various ways, it fully accepts that God who gave revelations to Moses and Jesus and is worshipped by Jews and Christians is none other than God who revealed the Qur'ān to Muḥammad and is worshipped by Muslims.

The traditional Christian view was that the Qur'ān and Muslims generally, in speaking of *Allāh*, are speaking of God. In 1734 George Sale, following the great Italian scholar Ludovico Marracci (who was also confessor of Pope Innocent XI), wrote:

> That both Mohammed and those among his followers who are reckoned orthodox, had and continue to have just and true notions of God and his attributes (always excepting their obstinate and impious rejecting of the Trinity), appears so plain from the Koran itself and all the Mohammedan divines, that it would be loss of time to refute those who suppose the God of Mohammed to be different from the true God . . .[3]

It would be interesting to study the history of the word 'Allah' in English and other European languages. It may owe something to the romantic conceptions of the orient which became fashionable about 1800, but more is probably due to the study of comparative religion in the later nineteenth century. In his lecture on Muḥammad in 1840 Thomas Carlyle occasionally used 'Allah', though usually when purporting to be giving Muḥammad's words or thoughts; mostly he spoke of 'God' and did not imply that Allah was other than God. On the other hand, in his life of Muḥammad published in 1932, the Swedish scholar Tor Andrae always speaks of 'Allah'; and, though he allows that this is a 'conception of God', seems to imply that it is different from the Jewish and Christian conceptions.[4] By this time, of course, it was becoming common among Christians to retain the name 'Yahweh' in

Old Testament passages instead of translating it as 'the Lord'.

In the present century it has become common for Muslims also to use 'Allah' instead of 'God' in English (and other European languages). 'Allah' is retained in Marmaduke Pickthall's translation of the Qur'ān, first published in 1930 with the approval of Egyptian Muslim authorities. It may be that this usage has been adopted as a way of emphasizing that Islam has a distinct identity from Judaism and Christianity and a distinctive conception of God. Yet the point must be treated with care. To say that Muslims worship Allah and Christians God is, from one point of view, like saying that the Germans worship Gott and the French Dieu. It has to be remembered, too, that there are several million Arabic-speaking Christians in Egypt, the Lebanon and elsewhere who have no other word for God than *Allāh*; and there were also pre-Islamic pagans who worshipped *Allāh*.

Whatever the motives of those who try to distinguish between 'Allah' and 'God', there is an important truth underlying their views. There are undoubtedly differences between Jewish, Christian and Muslim conceptions of God, even if the differences are less than appears at first sight. What is doubtful, however, is whether the use of different names is the best way of expressing these differences, since it must also be maintained that Jews, Christians and Muslims are worshipping and serving the same Being. One does not worship and serve a conception but a Being. When a man and woman marry, each has a conception of the other. After twenty years of married life the conceptions will be rather different; but they remain married to one another, since marriage is to a person, not to a conception. Similarly worship and service is a relation to a Being, not to a conception; and Jews, Christians and Muslims, though their conceptions differ, worship the same Being.

II The evocative character of the terms applied to God

It is impossible for human beings to speak of God without using anthropomorphic, that is, human, terms. Both the Bible and the Qur'ān speak of God as having a face, hands and other physical attributes. Non-physical attributes, like purpose and will, are also ascribed to God, and, since God is a spiritual Being, might seem to be used in a primary or literal sense. Reflection shows, however, that God's purpose and will are necessarily different from any human purpose and will, since he is eternal and in some sense above and beyond the temporal process. As the Qur'ān (42.11) puts it, 'like him is nothing' (*laysa ka-mithli-hi shay'*). For both Christianity and Islam, then, all the names and attributes of God (with one possible exception, to be considered presently) are 'symbolic' in the sense defined in the previous chapter.

Within Islam the philosophical or more rational theologians insisted that God could not be corporeal, and they branded those who understood literally terms like face and hand as Mushabbiha, 'those who likened (God to man)', or Mujassima, 'those who ascribed (to God) a body'. They themselves, on the other hand, interpreted such terms metaphorically. In the twelfth century the philosopher Ibn-Ṭufayl went so far as to regard anthropomorphic language as suitable only for the masses of ordinary people who could not understand the abstract terms of the philosophers. Other theologians, however, less philosophically-minded, adopted the doctrine of *balkafiyya* or 'amodality', according to which the anthropomorphic terms are to be accepted 'amodally' (*bi-lā kayf*), that is, without asking whether they are to be taken literally or metaphorically (cf. p. 3 above). This doctrine may well express the attitude of many ordinary Muslims (and also of many ordinary Christians in earlier centuries), who, without being able to formulate their attitude, did in practice accept terms 'amodally'; this is in contrast to modern Westerners, who in many respects are very literal-minded. It may also be noted that among Muslims were many ṣūfīs who had as a moral ideal 'being characterized by the characters (or attributes) of God' (*at-takhalluq bi-akhlāq Allāh*). The philosophical theologian al-Ghazālī discusses the matter in his book on the names of God, and justifies the phrase only with difficulty.[5]

The problem of anthropomorphic terms was also discussed by Christian theologians. The most famous solution was Thomas Aquinas' doctrine of 'analogy'. According to this, when terms are used of both God and human beings, they are neither univocal nor equivocal, that is, they are not used in the same sense, nor are they used in two completely unrelated senses. In other words, there is some relationship between the sense of the term as applied to God and its sense as applied to men, and this may be called 'analogy' but it cannot be precisely defined. Thus the anthropomorphic terms applied to God do not give an exact description but only hints or suggestions. In this respect they are evocative and not descriptive (cf. p. 3). When speaking about God it is important to remember that the symbolic terms used have this merely evocative character.

Consideration of 'the names and attributes of God' has a more central place in Islamic theology than in Christian, even though it is not wholly neglected by the latter. Many verses of the Qur'ān end with a phrase including two of these names of God, such as: 'He is the Knower, the Wise', 'He is the Forgiving, the Merciful'; and the standard invocation of God in Islam (the *basmala*) is 'In the name of God, the Compassionate, the Merciful'. In the course of time there arose the devotion of 'the Ninety-nine Most Beautiful Names', which are repeated while passing the beads of a rosary (*subḥa*) through the fingers.[6] The 'names' (*asmā'*) are mostly adjectival, and the corresponding abstract nouns constitute the 'attributes' (*ṣifāt*); thus to *raḥīm*, 'merciful', corresponds *raḥma*, 'mercy', and to *qādir*, 'powerful, (omni)potent', *qudra*, 'power, (omni)potence'.

It was mentioned above that there is one of the names of God which is possibly not symbolic. This is the name *God* itself in English, which is held to come from a Teutonic root meaning 'worship by sacrifice'. It is curious, however, that obscurity surrounds the etymology of the corresponding words in certain other languages, such as *Allāh* in Arabic and *theos* in Greek. This is not the place to discuss the etymologies, but only to consider what is involved in the application to God of a non-symbolic term. There are two possibilities with regard to the words in question. Firstly, it may prove to be the case that they are derived in some obscure way from a common primary word. Thus the name of the Greek god *Zeus* is held to be derived from the Aryan root for sky or day, indicating that he was a sky-god; and from the same root might come the Latin *deus* and perhaps even the Greek *theos*. In so far as this is so, then the word as applied to God is symbolic. Secondly, it is possible that the word in its original or root form referred to an experience—we might call it an experience of the numinous—for which in a particular culture there was a primary word. This would imply a limited cultural context within which the experience was frequent and specific, and so was clearly recognizable by observers within the culture. There was something of this recognizable character about the early Christian experience of receiving the Holy Spirit, for Peter, reporting to his fellow-apostles, said: 'as I began to speak, the Holy Spirit fell on them, as on us at the beginning'.[7] We might further suppose that, as the local culture was merged in a wider culture, the specific form of numinous experience might become less frequent or even be wholly replaced by other forms, yet the word would be retained. For Muslims and Christians today this means that the meaning of the word *God* in English and *Allāh* in Arabic is determined not by its original meaning, but partly by the experiences of the Islamic and

Christian communities through the centuries, and partly by their personal experiences.

III Certain attributes of God

(a) Oneness or unicity

The first half of the Islamic Shahāda or Confession of Faith asserts that 'there is no deity but God' (*lā ilāha illā llāhu*). (The first noun here, *ilāh*, is a common noun and should be translated as such; that is, in English 'deity' or 'god' not 'God'.) The oneness of God in this sense, which may also be expressed by 'unicity', was not emphasized in the earliest passages of the Qur'ān, but appeared early in the Meccan period. It marked the contrast between the belief of Muslims and that of the pagans who acknowledged *Allāh* as creator but also worshipped other gods. Muslims also hold that God is one in the sense of being a unity or whole without parts, but this did not prevent Muslim theologians from asserting that he had a multiplicity of attributes. Some of the arguments in this field, which now appear to be hair-splitting, were doubtless important when first propounded; e.g. when it was asked whether God knows by his *dhāt*, 'essence', or by his *'ilm*, 'knowledge'. At some periods Ash'arite and other theologians spoke of seven main attributes: power (omnipotence), knowledge (omniscience), will, speech, hearing, seeing, life. The Ash'arites insisted that these were 'not God and not other than God'—an interesting example of the evocative use of negative language. This problem of the attributes arose from the fact that in the main stream of Islamic thought the Qur'ān is accepted as the speech of God, and so as sharing in his eternity, although it clearly also has some sort of distinct existence. Opponents of those who held such views could say that they believed in 'two eternals', but despite this difficulty the Ash'arite doctrine of the attributes was vigorously maintained.

Christians also believe in the unicity of God, one of their main statements of belief, the Nicene Creed, opening with the words 'I believe in one God'. At the same time, however, they also believe that God is in some way threefold. The doctrine of the Trinity, as it is called, is subtle and abstruse, and most ordinary Christians simply accept it without being able to explain it fully. The usual English formulation is that there is 'one substance and three persons', which is based on the Latin terms *substantia* and *persona*. The use of the word 'person' in English is particularly confusing, because the normal sense of the word now is one which appeared only about the nineteenth century and was not intended by the sixteenth-century translators.[8] The Latin *persona* means 'an actor's mask, or a character in a play, or a role'. To avoid confusion it is often better to use the word employed for the three in Greek, namely, hypostasis. The Arabic *uqnūm* also avoids misleading connotations.

It is commonly thought that the Qur'ān criticizes the doctrine of the Trinity, but this is not necessarily so. Any statement about the matter requires to be carefully qualified. One of the verses dealing with the point is 5.73: 'disbelieved have those who say God is the third of three; there is no deity except one deity'. Taken literally this verse is criticizing belief in three gods, not in three hypostases; and from a Christian point of view belief in three gods is a heresy, tritheism. Throughout the centuries there have probably been simple-minded and badly instructed Christians whose effective belief may in fact have been tritheism, and there may well have been some such people in Arabia in Muḥammad's time. In so far as this is so and the Qur'ān is attacking tritheism, it is attacking a Christian heresy and orthodox Christians would agree with its criticisms.[9]

In the earlier centuries of the Islamic era some of the Christian theologians living in the Islamic world and writing in Arabic compared the Christian hypostases with the Islamic attributes. One suggestion, probably due to the Baghdad philosopher Yaḥyā ibn 'Adī (d. 974), was that the hypostases represented goodness, wisdom and power.[10] An alternative suggestion was that they were existence, speech and life;[11] some later Muslim theologians added existence and other attributes to the original seven. Yet a third version is mentioned by the Muslim intellectual historian ash-Shahrastānī (d. 1153) in his account of Christian doctrine; this consists of existence, knowledge and life.[12] That these attempts to find parallels should have been made is historically interesting, but they are remote from our contemporary concerns. It will be found in a later chapter that the differences between Christianity and Islam are not so much in this metaphysical field as in matters affecting the relationship of God and man.

(b) Transcendence and immanence

These two attributes may conveniently be dealt with together. Strictly speaking, they are contradictory of one another, but since, as applied to God, they are symbolic and evocative, the contradiction is only apparent. To transcend is to climb across or beyond something, and to be immanent is to remain in something. Since both 'beyond' and 'in' are spatial, they cannot be used in a primary sense of God, who is incorporeal .

Islam and Christianity may be said to agree that God is transcendent, although there is no word in Bible or Qur'ān that means precisely transcendent. God is somehow 'beyond' and 'above' his creation, not wholly contained in it. Isaiah in a vision (6.1) saw him 'sitting on a throne, high and lifted up', and also spoke of him (57.15) as 'the high and lofty One that inhabits eternity, whose name is Holy'. These terms, derived from the imagery of human kingship and majesty, have close parallels in Islam. One of the common terms in the Qur'ān is *rabb*, usually translated 'lord' but more adequately expressed by 'sovereign'. God is also said (7.54, etc.) to have seated himself on the throne (*'arsh*), which is above the heavens. Islam also emphasizes another aspect of transcendence, namely, God's difference from men (*mukhālafa*), and insists that anthropomorphic terms cannot be applied to God in the literal sense. There is a biblical parallel to this in a passage from Isaiah (55.8,9): 'for my thoughts are not your thoughts, neither are your ways my ways, says the Lord; for as the heavens are higher than the earth, so are my ways higher than your ways, and my thoughts than your thoughts'.

The Islamic conception of God's transcendence might seem to exclude any possibility of his immanence, but this is not so. There is a sense in which, according to the Qur'ān, God acts through men. Some Muslim theologians at a later date went so far as to say that men's acts were not really their acts but God's acts. This was not generally accepted in this extreme formulation, but there is some justification for it in the verse of the Qur'ān (8.17) relating to the battle of Badr which says: 'You [Muslims] did not kill them, but God killed them; and you [Muḥammad] did not shoot [arrows] when you shot, but God shot.'[13] God is also said to be nearer to man 'than his jugular vein' (50.16). A poem probably from the lifetime of Muḥammad speaks of five men returning from the killing of an opponent and so convinced of the rightness of their action that, the poet adds, 'and God was the sixth of us'.[14] This last shows that believers could be aware that God despite his transcendence was somehow present with them.

The conception of God's immanence in the world and in human activities is more at home in Christianity, notably in the doctrine of the incarnation (of which something will be said in chapter 7). Apart from this doctrine, God is spoken of as active in and through his creatures. In the Old Testament (as will be seen more fully in chapter 6) he strengthens men's hands to fight and gives victory to those who believe in him. In the New Testment we find Paul as he preaches at Athens saying that God 'is not far from every one of us, for in him we live and move and have our being' (Acts 17.27, 28). Paul also said that 'God was in Christ reconciling the world to himself' (2 Corinthians 5.19).

Since the words expressing or implying transcendence and immanence are only evocative, the differences between Islam and Christianity with regard to immanence, apart from the doctrine of incarnation, are relatively slight. It is probable, however, that both religions will have to face serious questions in dialogue with Hinduism and Buddhism where the Islamic and Christian distinction between objective and subjective is transformed and the possibility emerges that our apparently objective statements may themselves be in some way symbolic—a topic which cannot be pursued further here. More will have to be said, however, about transcendence and immanence in discussing God's activity in the natural universe and in human history (chapters 5 and 6).

(c) Love and goodness

Both Islam and Christianity have much to say about God's goodness. In the earlier passages of the Qur'ān there are many references to 'signs' (*āyāt*), that is, signs in natural events or objects of God's power and goodness.[15] Taken together, these show that God has made the world a place in which human beings can live in at least moderate comfort. The standard Muslim invocation of God, too, is as 'the Compassionate, the Merciful'; and among the other 'beautiful names' are 'the very Loving' (*wadūd*) and 'the constant Giver' (*wahhāb*). For Christianity, there are numerous references in the Old Testament to God's mercy, while in the New Testament a central theme is God's love for people in sending Jesus to them. God's love may be said to be the main topic of the First Epistle of John, and a climax is reached with the assertion 'God is love' (4.8, 16).

So far as names and words go there would seem to be little difference between Islam and Christianity. Nevertheless many Christians would claim that God as conceived by Christians is *more* loving than God as conceived by Muslims. For Christians, he is not merely benevolent towards those who obey and love him, but he is like a shepherd who goes out to look for and rescue sheep that have gone astray.[16] In the Qur'ān God has certainly loved all humanity in that he has sent to each community a prophet-messenger calling on them to serve God and appearing as a witness against them at the Last Judgment;[17] and in this way all humanity has had the opportunity of attaining to 'the great success' (*al-fawz al-'aẓīm*), which is the life of Paradise or Heaven. It is not clear, however, that those who serve God for a time and then turn away from him will be given a further chance. On the other hand, in the first century or so of Islam Muslims took Qur'ānic statements about the possibility of intercession (*shafā'a*) on the Last Day and developed the doctrine that Muḥammad would intercede for the sinners of his community; and it also came to be held that the intercession would be favourably received, so that these persons would eventually go to heaven, even though they might be punished for their sins, either in this life or for a limited period in hell. In this way Islam holds out some hope to those who have gone astray, although Christianity seems to place much more emphasis on God's active role in rescuing the lost.

Beliefs about God's love are probably reflected in the treatment of sinners and criminals. In this matter it is impossible to generalize, since there are many different attitudes within each religion. Many items of news in recent years have given Westerners the impression that Muslims are sterner and more rigorous in their punishment of offenders. Undoubtedly, however, there are many other Muslims whose attitudes are much more liberal. Among Christians, too, attitudes vary enormously. It is probably as a result of Christian influence that many Western states have abandoned the death penalty for murder; and yet there are also Christians who advocate more severe penalties for all sorts of offences and want the restoration of the death penalty. In this situation it is pointless to assign ratings to Islam and Christianity for their past performances. The essential question is what they are going to do from now onwards.

(d) Will and purpose

Terms like 'will' and 'purpose' are, of course, symbolic. The reason for mentioning these here is to call attention to an important difference in linguistic usage between Muslims and Christians. For Muslims, all that happens in the world is according to God's will; neither disaster nor good fortune can befall a man unless God wills it. In this usage even human sins are according to God's will. For Christians, on the other hand, God's will for men is what he wants them to do, that is, only good actions. Muslims express this Christian sense of 'the will of God' by speaking of 'the command of God'. Good actions are thus those commanded by God and of which he approves; they may also be said to be in accordance with his 'good pleasure' (*riḍā*).

Apart from the linguistic point the difference here is chiefly one of emphasis. Muslims place more emphasis on God's absolute control of all events, so that no evil can happen to anyone which is not in accordance with God's will. The common phrase on Arab lips ***in shā' Allāh***, 'if God will', with reference to future events, has a parallel in the Epistle of James (4.13-15): 'you who say, Today or tomorrow we will go into such a city and remain there a year, and buy and sell and get gain; although you do not know what shall be on the morrow . . . you ought to say, If the Lord will, we shall live and do this or that'. This is precisely the Muslim conception of God's will. Again, in Christian eyes, evils which happen to good men are regarded as 'the chastening of the Lord', for 'whom he loves he chastens' (Hebrews 12.5,6).

The precise nature of God's purpose or purposes will be discussed more fully at a later stage. Here it will be sufficient to note that God's will or purpose for the future must not be thought of as a precise plan or blue-print. Both Christians and Muslims maintain that the sinner by his sin cannot thwart God's purposes; but this does not mean that he cannot alter the course of events. He may or may not do so; but, if he does so, his sinful act will in some way or other be made part of the realization of God's purposes, though the exact form of the realization would have been different had he not sinned.

Chapter 4

Scripture as the word of God

Muslims and Christians are both, to use an Islamic phrase, 'peoples of the book', that is, adherents of a religion which has a written scripture, respectively the Qur'ān and the Bible. This is therefore something which the two communities have in common. In matters of detail, however, there are countless differences, and these will be described in the present chapter.

I Revelation and prophethood

The term 'revelation' will be taken as rendering the Arabic *waḥy* and *tanzīl*. The words are all symbolic, but the primary meanings are different. 'Revelation' means God's 'showing' or 'unveiling' of himself. *Tanzīl* is his 'sending down' of messages from heaven to earth. *Waḥy*, which became the technical Islamic word for 'revelation', is not much used except in this special sense, and it is difficult to know what its primary meaning is. In S. 19.11 *awḥā* (verb) is used of Zacharias when struck dumb and apparently means 'beckoned' or 'indicated by a sign'. In both religions what is revealed is also called 'the word of God'. The Arabic term is *kalām*, and this would be more correctly translated 'speech', since it is also used for God's attribute of speech, while a single word is represented by *kalima* (which is incidentally used of Jesus in S. 3.45; 4.171). Despite this slight linguistic difference it must be allowed that the phrase *kalām Allāh* plays much the same role in Muslim thinking as 'the word of God' in Christian thinking (apart from its application to Jesus).

Both Muslims and Christians thus believe that God speaks to people through individuals called 'prophets'. The initiative is always God's, as can be seen from the accounts of the calling of various prophets in the Old Testament and from the Islamic account of Muḥammad's call. In the Second Epistle of Peter (1.21) this is clearly stated: 'the prophecy came not in the old time by the will of man, but holy men of God spoke as they were moved by the Holy Spirit'. In accordance with English usage, Muḥammad will here be spoken of as 'prophet', although the commoner term for him in Arabic is *rasūl Allāh*. The Qur'ān has two words of roughly the same meaning, *nabī* and *rasūl*. The former is cognate with the Hebrew word for 'prophet' in the Old Testament. A *rasūl* is 'someone sent' and so may be translated 'messenger' or 'apostle'. Some later Muslim writers restricted *rasūl* to a man who had been commissioned by God to go to a particular community with his messages and to be its leader, whereas both the messengers and all those who had received any sort of communication from God, even by a dream, were 'prophets'. There was a statement to the effect that there were 315 messengers but 124,000 prophets.

Some of the statements about prophets in the Qur'ān suggest that the messages they received were assertions about God of a general kind, and all are held to have proclaimed the same message in essentials. Actually, however, many of the messages in the Qur'ān are instructions for dealing with particular situations. This point is indeed implicit in the Islamic conception of *asbāb an-nuzūl*, 'occasions of revelation'. These are items of information specifying the particular circumstances in which a certain passage was revealed. There are many such items of information, sometimes contradicting one another, and they do not cover the whole of the Qur'ān. So far as they go, however, they are helpful, although they are not part of the revelation. Sometimes, when there was a change in the situation in which Muslims found themselves, there had to be a change in the instructions. This is the basis of the doctrine of 'abrogation' (*an-nāsikh wa-l-mansūkh*), according to which certain commands or rules are retained in the text of the Qur'ān but are not obligatory because they have been replaced by others. Thus at Mecca Muḥammad was encouraged to spend much of the night in prayer, but at Medina he was told not to do this so that he might deal adequately with his daytime responsibilities (S. 73.1-7, 20). In *Muhammad at Mecca* I tried to show that the early passages as a whole were specially relevant to conditions in Mecca in the early seventh century AD.

Christians are probably more ready than Muslims to admit that prophetic messages are in the first place directed to the prophet's contemporaries in their particular circumstances. This is clearly the case with many of the Old Testament prophets, since they gave specific advice to their kings about political matters. Christians, however, would also maintain that what originally is relevant to a particular situation may also have universal relevance, since features of a particular situation may also be found in many other situations. Thus a particular reference does not exclude universal validity.

There are differences between the two religions about what Muslims call 'the manners of revelation' (*kayfiyyāt al-waḥy*). Three of these 'manners' are described in S. 42.51: 'It was not [fitting] for a man that God should speak to him except in *waḥy* or from behind a veil or that he should send a messenger who would by his permission make revelation [*awḥā*].' The detailed interpretation of these manners need not concern us here, but the third is more exactly described in S. 2.97: 'Gabriel . . . caused it to come down on your heart by God's permission.' Other manners are described in the Qur'ān and in Ḥadīth. Muslims have come to hold that the normal manner was for Muḥammad to receive the revelations through the angel Gabriel. The question has not attracted much attention from Christians in recent times. Samuel as a child heard God speaking to him (1 Samuel 3). Amos (7.14, 15) described his call thus: 'I was no prophet but a shepherd . . . and the Lord took me as I followed my flock and the Lord said to me, Go, prophesy to my people Israel.' Isaiah (6.1-13) saw a vision of God on a lofty throne and heard his voice speaking to him. Jeremiah (1.2,4) spoke of the word of the Lord 'coming to him' or 'being addressed to him'. In the historical account of the confrontation between a true prophet and false prophets, the former alleges that God 'has put a lying spirit in the mouth of the prophets', but it also seems to be implied that 'the spirit of God speaks' to true prophets (1 Kings 22.19-24). The commonest 'manner' in the Old Testament thus appears to be that the prophet hears God speaking to him, and the phrase 'Thus says the Lord' is common in the prophetic books.

If Christians are to speak of 'manners of revelation' in respect of the Bible, then they have to introduce some new 'manners'. In the Qur'ān every word is the word of God, and is comparable to what is found in the Bible along with the phrase 'Thus says the Lord'. The Bible also, however, contains material of many other kinds, since it is really a whole library of books dating from many different centuries. In the present context it will be sufficient to speak of historical material and epistolary material, though these categories together with prophecies do not exhaustively describe the contents of the Bible. Christians regard all the books of the Bible as part of God's revelation of himself, but they tend to speak of the writers of the books, other than the prophets, not as having 'received revelations' but as being 'inspired', that is, as having been guided in their writing by God's spirit, the Holy Spirit. It is generally held that the writers were inspired even when they were incorporating earlier written material (as seems to have happened in the historical books of the Old Testament and in the Gospels); in some cases, of course, this earlier material could also have been produced by inspired writers. Whatever the course of composition, the books as we now have them bring us truth from God and show us how God deals with men. More will be said about this in chapter 6. A slightly different form of inspiration would seem to be present in the epistles or letters collected in the New Testament. Because the writers had shared in the early experiences of the Church and had important places in it, they might be said to have received a gift of divine wisdom through which their letters come to contain God's truth.

The use of the word 'inspiration' has to be looked at carefully. Both 'inspire' and 'spirit' are derived from the Latin *spiro*, 'I breathe', and thus have some similarities with the Arabic *rūḥ*. The term 'inspiration', however, is commonly used to translate the Arabic *ilhām*. Apart from a single use of this word in the Qur'ān, where the interpretation is much disputed, it is commonly applied by Muslims to a form of communication of divine truth to saints and holy persons. This differs from *waḥy*, 'revelation', in that it does not consist of messages for the whole community but only of private messages for the individuals receiving it, even though for them it may be a true basis for action. Christians would certainly claim that what they have in the non-prophetic books of the Bible is closer to *waḥy* than to *ilhām*, and is truth from God of universal validity.

It has sometimes been suggested that the historical books of the Bible are comparable to the collections of Ḥadīth in Islam. The Ḥadīth – in older Western books usually called 'traditions' – are anecdotes about the sayings and doings of Muḥammad. There are many thousands of these, and six of the important collections have a kind of canonical status for legal purposes. Thus they constitute an additional or secondary scripture in Islam. There is an important difference, however, between these and the historical material in Christian scripture. Ḥadīth have a revelational quality because they embody the wisdom (*ḥikma*) given to Muḥammad by God. Ash-Shāfiʿī (d. 820), who is the founder of the

Islamic discipline of 'principles of jurisprudence' (*uṣūl al-fiqh*), quoted a verse (4.113) which says that God has sent down on Muḥammad the Book and the Wisdom (*ḥikma*), and maintained that this Wisdom is expressed in the practice (*sunna*) of Muḥammad as recorded in the Ḥadīth.[1] It was also required that each anecdote should be authenticated by an *isnād*, that is, a list of those who had transmitted it either orally or in writing; but all that was demanded of the transmitters was that they should be honest and upright and have good memories. There was thus no suggestion that those who transmitted or wrote down Ḥadīth should be inspired in any way. For Christians on the other hand, the writers of historical books must be more than truthful reporters of what they have heard or seen; they must be personally 'inspired'.

There are many problems here worthy of further thought and study; for example, how far were the historical writers dependent on the prophets' way of regarding events, as when a prophet said, 'In this disaster God was punishing the Israelites for worshipping other deities'? Let us leave such problems aside, however, and concentrate on the general question of how these 'manners' are related to the content of the revelation. The 'manners' might be described as the ways in which the prophet (or inspired writer) experienced the receiving of divine truth. In the case of the prophets, one might speak of the imaginal or perceptual form, which could be auditory or visual or both or neither; that is, he might hear words or see a vision or both, or simply find words in his consciousness. The imaginal form possibly depended in part on temperament, and it was certainly important for the prophet himself. It was one of the factors which gave him a confident belief that he had really received a revelation from God; and it was necessary for him to have this confident belief if he was to carry on his work of proclaiming the revealed messages in the face often of considerable opposition. The fact that a prophet might receive revelations in several different 'manners' is not a problem, since many of the terms in the descriptions are to be understood in a symbolic and evocative sense. This is also true of the conception of 'angel'; though angels are not recognized by science, there is nothing in the cosmological scheme to be presented in the next chapter which makes the existence of angels impossible; but the term cannot be more than evocative. Ultimately the way in which revelation comes to a prophet is a mystery, but we can be certain of two things: (a) it is God who takes the initiative in revelation; and (b) the form of words in the consciousness of the prophet contains truth from God.

While the 'manner' may serve as the first criterion of the truth of the message, it has to be supplemented by another. In the story mentioned above from 1 Kings 22 the false prophets believed that the spirit of God was speaking through them and doubted whether the spirit was speaking through the man regarded as a true prophet by the writer; and thus being addressed by the spirit is not a sufficient criterion. In recent times in the West there have been people who tried to associate claims to receive messages from God with some pathological physical or mental condition in the recipient. Even if such a condition could be proved to exist in a particular person, however, it would not prove the claim either false or true. God may, if he will, work through persons with strange types of temperament. Ultimately, however, the claims to truth of a general system of revelation (not of particular items) must be tested by the criterion of 'fruits',[2] that is, the quality of life of those who, following the prophet, make this system of revelation the basis of all their conduct. This criterion can be and is applied both by the committed followers of the prophet themselves and by non-committed observers.

The purpose of revelation is to give men a view of reality in respect of God's being and attributes and the mutual relations of God and men; that is, it shows God's goodness and power, his sovereignty over the world, his control of historical events, what he demands of men and how men may set about trying to fulfil these demands, together with the rewards of success in this and the penalties of failure. It is not the purpose of revelation to give men scientific knowledge or information about purely factual aspects of history, though it does present historical events as showing something about the relations of God and men. To suppose that the scriptures give a *scientific* theory (called 'creationism' in America) of the origin of the world is a misunderstanding of the purpose of revelation. This is a very important point.

After all these considerations what have Christians to say about the prophethood of Muḥammad? For Muslims, of course, Jesus is a prophet, and indeed something more than a prophet, since the Qur'ān (4.171) speaks of him as 'God's word which he put into Mary and a spirit from him'. For Christians the question of Muḥammad's prophethood is more difficult, especially with the continuing influence in some minds of the medieval caricatures. In the light of the above discussions the following seem to be the salient points. Muḥammad claimed to receive messages from God and conveyed these to his contemporaries. On the basis of these messages a religious community developed, claiming to serve God, numbering some thousands in Muḥammad's lifetime, and now having several hundred million members. The quality of life in this community has been on the whole satisfactory for the members. Many men and women in this community have attained to saintliness of life, and countless ordinary people have been enabled to live decent and moderately happy lives in difficult circumstances. These points lead to the conclusion that the view of reality presented in the Qur'ān is true and from God, and that therefore Muḥammad is a genuine prophet.

II The human element in revelation

Muslims tend to think that because a revelation is the word of God there is nothing human in it. Because of the different character of most of the Bible from the Qur'ān and its different literary history – in the case of the Qur'ān its 'collection' – Christians have been more aware of the human element in revelation, especially during the last century. Yet there is also a human element in the Qur'ān as a little reflection shows. Nothing to be said in what follows, however, is in contradiction to the two points just made, namely, that in revelation the initiative is God's, and that the form of words constituting the scriptures contains and expresses truth from God.

There is something paradoxical in the idea that written or spoken words may be the word or speech of God. Because God is eternal and transcendent he can be known to man only in so far as he reveals himself to man. If this self-revelation of God is to be in language, that means that God must restrict it to those aspects of his being which may be expressed in human, creaturely language with all its imperfections; and even here God accepts the limitations on what he can communicate to men through this medium. Some Muslim theologians seem to have been aware of this problem, because when speaking of the Qur'ān as written or spoken, they said, not that it was the speech of God, but that it was an *'ibāra* or *dalāla* or *ḥikāya* or *rasm* of the Qur'ān – words which seem to mean something like 'expression' or 'indication' or 'reproduction'.[3] These general difficulties are increased when certain points are looked at in detail.

Since a prophet is sent to a specific people, the revealed messages must be in language understood by these people. Language, however, is a human construction. It can indeed be said that it is created by God, but this is only in the sense in which God gives men bread, yet through human work, and it still leaves language as something created. Moreover, languages differ greatly from one another, not only in actual vocabulary but even in the categories of thought implied in this vocabulary. This was briefly mentioned above.[4] A Christian theologian, Leslie Dewart, has studied the differences between Arabic and Greek (and other languages) in how they express such ideas as 'essence' and 'existence', noting, for example, that the Arabic word for 'existent' properly means 'found';[5] and he has suggested that 'the concrete, determinate form of any philosopical doctrine may sometimes be determined by the structure of the language (or languages) in which philosophers think'.[6] Such differences between languages give some justification for holding that revealed scriptures cannot be adequately translated from their original language. Yet human beings somehow or other have to try to understand one another across language barriers.

Not merely does a language have its distinctive categories of thought, but it also enshrines the whole view of reality at any period of those who use the language, including their views on cosmology and history. In the case of the Arabs at the time of Muḥammad's call, their ideas about cosmology and general history were rudimentary. They knew a little about the past of Arabia and Mecca, and they were familiar with bedouin customs. It is worth considering the linguistic problem involved in communicating to people with such a background the Islamic doctrine of God, one, eternal and transcendent. They were familiar with the word *Allāh*, but it did not mean to them what it now means to a Muslim. Some were certainly pagans who believed in *Allāh* as 'high god' and creator, but also as only one god among many even if superior to them. There were Jews and Christians, too, at Mecca and Medina, who may have used *Allāh* for 'God' when speaking Arabic. Much teaching was thus needed before Muḥammad's followers could fully appreciate the Islamic conception of God. It may be because of this difficulty about the word *Allāh* that it is rare in the early suras (apart from the *basmala*); much commoner is the designation 'your lord' (*rabbu-ka*), which is less likely to be misunderstood.

A relatively unimportant matter on which cosmological ideas affect the wording of the Qur'ān are those verses where God is spoken of as spreading out the earth for men.[7] It is virtually certain that the Arabs of Muḥammad's time thought that the earth was not spherical but a great flat expanse. To such persons a verse like 2.22, 'who made the earth a bed for you', would obviously suggest the flatness of the earth; and without asking any questions they would understand it in terms of their inherited cosmological ideas. In other words, revelation is necessarily expressed in terms of existing cosmology. It would have been impossible through revealed messages to persuade these Arabs that the earth was a sphere; and in any case to do so would have served no religious purpose. The matter only became of practical importance when men circumnavigated the globe or made other lengthy journeys. What the Qur'ān teaches in S. 2.22 and other verses is that God has made the earth a suitable place for human life. It is interesting to note that later Muslim commentators like al-Bayḍāwī (d. 1286), who knew the earth to be spherical, pointed out that, although this was so, it appeared to be flat like a bed because of its great extent.

To consider that the earth is flat is an approximation rather than a mistake, since a limited part of its surface, like a large lake, may be thought of as flat for most human purposes. There may be other matters, however, where the intellectual outlook of the recipients of revelation is definitely mistaken. For example, there is a slight mathematical mistake in the Bible, where it speaks of a large circular basin, called a 'sea', which is ten cubits across and thirty cubits round (2 Chronicles 4.2); actually a circle which is ten units in diameter has a circumference of over thirty-one units. Presumably the people for whom this was written were accustomed to work with this low degree of accuracy, and it was not part of the purpose of scripture to change their outlook in such matters. In similar fashion, some of the verses in which Western scholars have alleged that the Qur'ān has made mistakes, should be regarded as being expressed in terms of mistaken views current among the people of Mecca and Medina. Examples are the address to Mary, mother of Jesus, as 'sister of Aaron' (19.28), and the apparent denial of the crucifixion of Jesus (4.157). It is probable that there were people in Arabia who had such ideas, and it was not part of the purpose of revelation to correct them. With regard to the crucifixion it is known that there were certain Christian heretics, called Gnostics, who denied that Jesus died on the cross. The primary purpose of S. 4.157 appears to be not to deny the death as such, but to deny that the bringing about of his death by the Jews was triumph for them (a point with which Christians could agree).

There are instances in the Bible of something like 'abrogation' as understood by Muslims. For example, after the fall of Jerusalem to the Babylonians in 587 BC and the assassination of the governor left in charge of the district a large party of the remaining Israelites decided to flee to Egypt. The prophet Jeremiah warned them that if they do so, 'they shall die by the sword, by the famine and by the pestilence, and none of them will remain or escape from the evil that I will bring on them there, says the Lord' (42.17). It appears, however, that a Jewish community continued to exist in Egypt, presumably including the descendants of these refugees. Again, the prophet Ezekiel about the same time, foretelling the fall of the city of Tyre, then head of a great empire, said that it would completely disappear before long; 'you shall be no more; though you are sought for, yet shall you not be found again' (26.21). In fact, though it was defeated by the Babylonians, its empire did not collapse until it was besieged by Alexander in 332 BC; and shortly after that the town was restored as a town and still exists. Yet again, about 520 BC, when some Jews had returned from Babylon to Jerusalem, the prophets Haggai and Zechariah spoke of the governor Zerubbabel in terms which implied that he was the Messiah and expressed high hopes for the future; but Zerubbabel somehow disappears from history, and the hopes were seriously disappointed.

It would be wrong to regard these prophecies as false. A passage in Jeremiah justifies the non-fulfilment of prophecies: God says,

> when I decree concerning a nation or a kingdom that I will pluck it up, pull it down and destroy it, if that nation . . . turns from its wickedness, I will repent of the evil I intended to do to it; and when I decree . . . that I will build and plant, if it does evil . . . I will repent of the good . . . (18.7-10)

These principles may be applied in a general way to the biblical instances given, although we do not know enough about the details to say definitely that there was some change of heart in the people in question. What can be said definitely, however, is that the words of the prophets stated truly how God normally acts in such situations. Thus it was right for the prophets to encourage the people to think of Zerubbabel as the Messiah, since if they accepted the belief and acted confidently, there was a possibility of carrying forward the restoration of Jerusalem. Some progress was achieved, but then owing to circumstances of which we are ignorant the work of restoration was halted.

A matter of a different kind is the occurrence of errors in the transmission of revelation. The simplest form of this is the occurrence of variants in the text of the scriptures. Since human beings are liable to make mistakes, and can be negligent and careless even when dealing with sacred things, it is not surprising that there are some variations when texts are copied by hand. Even in modern printed secular books, where great care is taken, a few printing errors usually creep in. What may be said in the case of the Bible and the Qur'ān, however, is that none of the variants significantly affects our understanding of the truths revealed.

In the case of the Qur'ān most of the variants can be explained in terms of the Ḥadīth that the Qur'ān was revealed according to seven 'readings' (*aḥruf*).[8] The deeper meaning of this Ḥadīth would seem to be that the variants in question do not significantly alter the sense of the revelation, since all are accepted. There are also, however, those variants known as pre-'Uthmānic, which were recorded and studied by medieval Muslim scholars.[9] The most interesting of these early variants is Ibn-Mas'ūd's reading of 'Ḥanīfiyya' instead of 'Islam' in S. 3.19.

Since the history of the 'collection' of the Bible is more complex than that of the Qur'ān and extends over a longer period of time, the variants are more numerous and sometimes also more substantial. One of the most significant is in the Marcan account of the healing of an epileptic demoniac, where Jesus is reported as saying (9.29): 'this kind comes out only by prayer', but with the variant '. . . only by prayer and fasting'. The latter was long accepted as the true text, but New Testament scholars now think that the former is more likely to be the true version. Muslims might think that this was a serious discrepancy, since it raises the question whether fasting is a necessary part of a healing ministry; but Christians have not regarded this as an important difference. Works of healing have occurred at the hands of some Christians through the centuries, but they would regard the saying of Jesus, in either form, only as making clear that deep spiritual preparation was needed on the part of the 'healer', not as specifying the precise nature of the preparation. This would depend on the 'healer's' individual temperament, and also perhaps on his cultural environment in such points as the attitude to fasting. Most 'healers' would presumably be men of prayer; but fasting would not necessarily be practised even by those who accepted the textual variant which mentioned fasting. This is incidentally an illustration of how the interpretation of texts is affected by experience, but the point to be emphasized here is that the existence of variant texts does not impair the believer's understanding of his faith.

Difficulty might also be felt by some believers because the four gospels in the New Testament vary in numerous details. A little reflection, however, shows that this difficulty is only apparent. If one considers an important person of recent times, such as Muḥammad

Iqbal, different friends and different readers of his works would form different conceptions of his personality. Yet in so far as these are based on genuine facts, they would all truly represent the man, though from different aspects, and they would thus complement one another to form a fuller portrait of him. It is impossible to give in words a full and complete picture of any human being, since the human personality is fuller and richer than any form of words can show. This applies to the four accounts of the work and personality of Jesus. If we take each as a whole, it presents a picture of him from a particular angle or viewpoint; and the four together thus give us a better conception of him than one alone could have done, even had it been much longer. In this case, then, the differences are not a defect, but make a positive contribution to our knowledge of Jesus.

A final question is whether the individual personality of the prophet affects in any way the form and content of the revelation made to him. The revelation is, of course, necessarily affected by the intellectual and cultural outlook of the community to which it is addressed, and in which the prophet shares. In addition, however, it would appear that the prophet would require to have a special kind of temperament to fit him to be a recipient of revelation, and this temperament might affect the 'imaginal form' of the revelation. Closely connected with the temperament of the prophet would be his spiritual quality, which might come in part from his temperament and in part from his assiduity in practising his religion. This again is to be distinguished from actual events in the prophet's life which may be taken up into the revelation, as when Ezekiel's wife dies and God tells him not to mourn for her in order to symbolize the depth of the tragedy which is overtaking Jerusalem; or as when Muḥammad is encouraged by being reminded of instances of God's goodness to him in his earlier life.[10] Rather different is the case of the prophet Hosea and his wife. When she went and prostituted herself, he was told to take her back, although she had been unfaithful to him, and to treat her kindly. This was to symbolize God's readiness to take back unfaithful Israel after it had 'committed adultery' by worshipping false gods (3.1-5). What is not clear is whether Hosea was of himself inclined to take his wife back and then was brought to see that this showed something of God's nature, or whether he did not think of taking her back until God told him to do so. Whatever view one takes of such matters, it remains true that revelation comes through God's initiative, that its content is his truth, and that the way in which it comes is a mystery.

III The acceptance of revelation

Not merely is there a human element *in* revealed scriptures because of their use of human language, but there is even more of a human element in the way in which a religious community accepts its scriptures, finds meaning in them and makes them part of its life and experience. While the scriptural text is in a sense objective, there is a subjective element in the meaning the community takes out of it.

Where common sense supposes that people are completely passive in understanding statements which they hear or read, philosophers are pretty well agreed that the human mind has to be active in this process of understanding, since it has to relate the new assertions to its previous knowledge. This includes both the meaning of individual words and people's whole conception of the world in which they live. As an example of an individual word one might take *Allāh*. The Qur'ān itself tells us that there were pagans in Mecca who acknowledged *Allāh* along with other deities, though considering him superior to the others. When such persons heard a revelation about *Allāh*, they would naturally suppose that it was about this 'high god' with whom they were familiar. They could not possibly understand the word as it was later understood by Muslims as a result of Qur'ānic teaching. This teaching, too, could only be given gradually. It is probably because of the likelihood of *Allāh* being misunderstood that it occurs only rarely in the earliest revelations, and the teaching is given in terms of 'your Lord' (Muḥammad's) or 'their Lord' and the like. One of the earliest usages of *Allāh* is probably that in S.95.8: 'Is not *Allāh* the justest of judges?'; and this clearly expresses one aspect of the Islamic conception of God. It was doubtless a long time before the Meccans were able to understand that the pagan deities were not merely inferior to *Allāh* (as they had thought) but were mere names without corresponding reality.

Once there is a considerable corpus of revelational material the question of selective emphasis arises. As people have to deal with the problems which occur in the course of their lives, they find that some passages are more helpful than others. Sedentary agriculturalists, for example, might be impressed by the passages in the Qur'ān which speak of the revival of 'dead' land by rain as a sign of resurrection. It is easy to pass from such selective emphasis to interpretation in the sense of drawing implications. On the basis of such Qur'ānic verses as 75.23, 'looking to their Lord', many Muslims came to regard the vision of God as one of the great joys of Paradise. This vision of God has also played an important part in Christian thought. Other Muslims, however, notably the Muʿtazilites, objected to the emphasis on such verses, because it apparently made God corporeal, and that contradicted a belief that was very important for them, namely, that God is incorporeal. This example shows how sectarian differences can emerge, a matter to be more fully considered in the next section.

After people have lived on the basis of scriptures for decades or centuries their actual experience becomes a factor in the interpretation of the scriptures. In the example given above of the Christian treatment of the variants, 'only by prayer' and 'only by prayer and fasting', experience was an important factor. This is another example of the use of the criterion of 'fruits' in judging religious belief and practice. People defend the interpretation of the scriptures which they follow, with any special emphasis, when they find that its 'fruits' in their experience are satisfying. As new circumstances arise and experience grows, the understanding of the scriptures becomes deeper. One might take as an example the expansion of the conception of Muḥammad's vocation as *rasūl Allāh*, 'Messenger of God'. Just as the pagan Meccans could not have understood *Allāh* in an Islamic sense, so Muḥammad at the beginning of his activity as prophet could not have understood the full implications of 'messenger of God'. For this reason (apart from others) the accounts of how Gabriel came to him and said 'You are the Messenger of God' can hardly be the original version of his call. Early passages of the Qur'ān (e.g. 74.2; 87.9) suggest that at first Muḥammad's vocation was described in terms of 'warning' and 'reminding', to which the corresponding nouns are 'warner' (*nadhīr*) and 'one reminding' (*mudhakkir*). It is also explicitly stated (88.21f.) that he is only a *mudhakkir*, not a *muṣayṭir* or 'overseer' over people. As the number of his followers grew, however, it became necessary for him to exercise some kind of leadership for them. One verse (72.23), generally accepted as Meccan, after saying that his function is only to communicate the messages (*risālāt*), goes on to speak of those who disobey God and his *rasūl*; but it is conceivable that the word *yaʿṣi* here means only acting contrary to what was said rather than disobeying an explicit command. After the *Hijra*, however, Muḥammad was not merely to be obeyed but also to have cases brought before him for judgment (24.47–52; 4.59), even though some of the men of Medina may have been reluctant to do this.[11] His successes in conquering Mecca and winning the battle of Ḥunayn greatly increased his authority in actual practice and made him head of a vast alliance. This meant that when he died in 632 the *rasūl* had so many responsibilities other than the conveying of God's messages that Abū-Bakr had to be appointed as his *khalīfa* or replacement in respect only of these non-prophetic duties. This is how the conception of the *rasūl* grew with changing circumstances.

Included in the experience of a religious community are its relationships to deviant groups within itself and to rival communities, and this aspect of its experience may also affect its scriptural interpretations. If at any time the main body feels that it is being threatened or endangered by deviants or rivals, it will feel that its own identity needs to be strongly asserted and so will favour polemical interpretations which strengthen its own position and weaken that of the opponents. On the other hand, if it feels that the age is one where the chief threat is from secular bodies and that the deviants or rivals are potential allies, it will look rather for some reconciliation with these groups and will favour eirenic interpretations of texts. Thus, even though the scriptural text is fixed, there can be a certain flexibility in interpretation. After the Islamic state had conquered Egypt, Syria and Iraq, where there were many educated Christians, Muslim scholars felt that the presence of these Christians might endanger the faith of ordinary Muslims, and so in order to protect them developed the theory of the corruption of the Christian (and Jewish) scriptures. The verses of the Qur'ān on which the theory is based are far from implying total corruption.[12] In present circumstances, when some Muslims feel that dialogue with Christians is desirable, it should be possible for them to produce an interpretation of these verses, which speak only of limited or perhaps temporary 'corruption'. Similarly, Christians might be expected to correct some of the false Qur'ānic interpretations associated with the distorted medieval image of Islam.

IV From scripture to dogma

The relation of the religious experience of a community to its scripture may be looked at from another angle, namely, that known to Christians as 'the formation of the canon of scripture'. This corresponds in some respects to the Islamic 'collection' of the Qur'ān, but there are also differences. These are due to the fact that the whole Qur'ān was revealed in just over twenty years, whereas the Christians had to deal with many separate 'works' produced over a period of a century or two—and this leaves aside the question of the books which the Christians share with the Jews. The Christian scholars had to deal with two main problems. Firstly, they had to distinguish between the genuine works of the first apostles, together with works based on their teachings, like the Second and Third Gospels, and many works written by members of deviant sects, especially the Gnostics, which were in some ways contrary to the true teaching of the apostles. Secondly, they had to distinguish those genuine works which were primary evidence of the revelation in and through Jesus from secondary works, which contained true teaching, but whose authors had not personally experienced the life of the Christian community in the period immediately after the resurrection. By insisting that the only true and basic Christian teaching was that contained in the works of the first apostles and the men associated with them the main body of Christians by the early fourth century had reached agreement about which books constituted the revealed scripture —the New Testament as we still have it.

The 'collection' of the Qur'ān was a much simpler affair, and under the caliph 'Uthmān about 650 the Muslims were content to leave the work to Zayd ibn-Thābit and three associates. The result they produced was universally accepted by Muslims, though the records of pre-'Uthmānic variants were not all destroyed. Some further work was required after the improvement of writing to distinguish more clearly between consonants and to indicate vowels. This led to the acceptance of the seven *aḥruf* (already mentioned) and to the consequent system of *qirā'āt* or 'sets of readings'. A greater resemblance to the formation of the New Testament canon is to be seen in the process by which the 'six books' of Ḥadīth came to have a superior status to other collections and might be called 'canonical'.[13] There was no official decision about this matter, but agreement was gradually achieved as more and more scholars acknowledged the superior merits of the 'six books'.

Once a community has definitely decided what is included in the corpus of its scriptures and what excluded, it is in a sense committed to the loyal acceptance of these scriptures, and this becomes an element in its identity. In the course of time, however, fresh problems arise, since not all passages in the scriptures are equally clear and equally important—a fact which is at the basis of the Islamic distinction, applied to verses of the Qur'ān, between *mutashābih*, 'ambiguous', and *muḥkam*, 'perfect' or 'precise'. Different groups emphasize different aspects or interpret doctrinal statements in different ways. The community has then to decide which views are in accordance with its general understanding of the scriptures and which contrary.

In the Christian Church in the fourth century a great controversy was stirred up by the views of a theologian called Arius. Though he was prepared to admit (following the opening verses of the Fourth Gospel) that the Word of God was God's agent in the creation of the world and was later incarnated in Jesus, he insisted that this Word was itself created. All the leading theologians of the time took part in the arguments, which lasted for over half a century. Eventually the main body decisively rejected the views of Arius as heretical, and slowly over centuries the Arians dwindled away. In order to make clear that the views of Arius were not in accordance with the scriptures brief formulations were added to the short creeds (doctrinal statements) used in baptisms. In its new form the creed made clear how the main body of Christians interpreted the scriptures on the point at issue. Other disputed points were dealt with similarly and new phrases added to the creed. Two such creeds are commonly used by Christians in worship, the Apostles' Creed and the Nicene Creed (or Creed of Nicaea).[14] These creeds have an official status, since they were approved by 'ecumenical councils' consisting of all Christian bishops throughout the *oikūmenē* or 'world' (i.e. the Greek and Roman world). The Nicene Creed was first formulated at the Council of Nicaea in 325 and was then approved in a slightly longer form at the Council of Constantinople in 381.

In Islam many of the leading thinkers formulated a creed (*'aqīda, 'aqā'id*). Some thirty are listed in the bibliography of the article ''Aḳīda' of the new edition of the *Encyclopaedia of Islam*, and there are many more. They vary greatly in length, and the longer ones should perhaps rather be called by another name. Like the Christian creeds they give a positive statement of the main doctrines of the faith, while at the same time excluding heresies, either by careful formulation of the doctrines or by explicit condemnation of the false view. Thus against the Mu'tazilites it was insisted by Aḥmad ibn-Ḥanbal and most Sunnites that the Qur'ān, which is the eternal word or speech of God, is not created. The Islamic creeds differ from the Christian, however, in two ways. They are not used in worship and they do not have any official status—this last because there is no Islamic institution corresponding to the 'ecumenical councils'. Nevertheless, among Sunnite Muslims there is general agreement on all the main credal doctrines. This has been reached in much the same way as agreement on the 'six books'. Some Islamic sects, like the Imāmites and the Ismā'ilites, have also produced creeds or statements of belief. In Christianity, besides the creeds, there have been longer statements of belief, some purely of an individual character, some with a degree of official approval.

It may also be noted that in Christianity the Apostles' and Nicene Creeds partly serve to define the identity of the community, in that the community is committed to loyal acceptance of them in the same way as it is committed to loyal acceptance of the canonical scriptures. In this respect the creeds may be regarded as expressing the quintessence of scripture. In them the basic doctrines are emphasized, and limits are indicated which are to be observed in the interpretation of scriptural texts. For example, because the creed says that Jesus was 'born of the Virgin Mary', the words spoken by Mary (Luke 2.48), 'your father and I have sought you sorrowing', must not be interpreted to mean that Joseph was the father of Jesus in a physical sense; he was only father in a 'social' sense as head of the family to which Jesus belonged and also thought of by other people as his father. Parallel to this position of the creeds in Christianity is the emphasis on 'orthodoxy', namely, on the fact that right intellectual belief is taken as a criterion of membership of the Church. The corresponding criterion in Islam is probably 'following the Sunna of the Prophet'.

V God's commands for human society

Both Christianity and Islam believe that God has given commands concerning the conduct of individuals in their relations with other people; certain acts are prescribed, other acts are forbidden, There is an important difference, however, in the practical experience of the two communities. Christianity accepted the commands given by God to Moses, of which the main ones are those in the Ten Commandments. There were many other rules, however, some more detailed, others very general, such as 'you shall love your neighbour as yourself' (Leviticus 19.18). These rules are collectively known to the Jews as the Torah, and from them Jewish rabbis produced a system of law in much the same way as Muslim ulema elaborated the Sharī'a. A form of this law was in force in the time of Jesus in Palestine, except in so far as it was overridden by Roman law. Jesus accepted the Mosaic law, but, following John the Baptist in this, criticized certain aspects of its contemporary application, notably the attaching of great importance to ritual matters and the like and the comparative neglect of some of the main ethico-legal conceptions. He also taught that bad intentions were sinful, even if not followed by bad actions.

Unlike the early Muslims the early Christians did not constitute a political entity or state, and so they had no responsibility for framing or administering laws. What they found, however, especially those of them who lived outside Palestine, was that in the Roman empire there was a system of law owing nothing to revelation, and yet roughly in accordance with the ethico-legal parts of the Mosaic law. When the Roman empire became officially Christian in the early fourth century it already had a system of law which was in general acceptable to Christians, and there was no need to create a new system of law based solely on the Mosaic law as modified by the teaching of Jesus. Living in the Roman empire made it clear to Christians that sound human reason, apart from revelation, could reach a satisfactory system of law. Thus in medieval Christendom and in modern Western Christendom until the present century, although the laws of the various states were expected to be in accordance with biblical teaching, it was not considered necessary to show how a particular law was derived from scriptural texts. In Protestant countries since the Reformation such matters have been left to the 'secular' discipline of moral philosophy, and for a long time this scheme worked well, since most of the moral philsophers were convinced Christians, or at least accepted Christian moral teaching. In the present century, however, there has been increased questioning of Christian beliefs and Christian morality, and there is now some uncertainty about the precise basis of Christian ethico-legal conceptions.

Islam was a political unit from the time of Muḥammad's Hijra to Medina, but it did not have to construct a system of law out of nothing. In general the customs of the nomadic Arabs prevailed even in the towns of Mecca and Medina, though in some respects the customary practices were not suited to urban life. Where there was something unsatisfactory, the Qur'ān gave new rules; but otherwise things went on as before. After Muḥammad's death, as the Islamic state grew into an empire, many influential Muslims came to think that the legal system of the empire (which was primarily only for Muslims, not for non-Muslims) should be based on the Qur'ān together with the Sunna or practice of Muḥammad. This last was necessary because the Qur'ānic rules covered only a limited number of matters, whereas the Sunna of Muḥammad showed the extent and the manner in which he had accepted traditional nomadic practices. The great jurist ash-Shāfi'ī (d. 820) produced a theory of 'the roots of law' (*uṣūl al-fiqh*) which gained wide agreement and showed how to determine the Sunna and how to apply the rules of the Qur'ān and Sunna to novel situations. He also held that in the Sunna was exemplified 'the widsom' (*ḥikma*) which God had given to Muḥammad according to the Qur'ān, so that Qur'ān and Sunna together were the basis of the Sharīʿa or God-given law. Thus in theory the only law of Islamic states is the Sharīʿa, and it should be possible to show that all enactments are in accordance with the Qur'ān and Sunna (as known from the Ḥadīth). The only exception in theory is that in some minor matters attention may be paid to local custom (*ʿurf, ʿāda*),[15] but in practice since the mid-nineteenth century many Islamic states have adopted laws based on European ideas.

The contrast between the Islamic belief that all laws should be based on God's commands and the Christian readiness to accept sound human reason as a source of law parallel to revelation is one of the greatest differences between the two religions, and raises the question whether in the future it will be possible for Muslims to co-operate in the field of law with Christians, or at least for the two to have some degree of mutual understanding. There are three important areas where it is desirable that there should be a common effort not merely by Muslims and Christians but also by the adherents of the other main systems of belief. These three areas are: the conduct of individuals; the conduct of states or other political units towards one another and towards their subjects; and the basis of authority of legal and moral ideals.

Firstly, in so far as law refers to the conduct of individuals in society Islam and Christianity are agreed on the fundamentals. The ethico-legal matters in the Ten Commandments are respect for life, respect for marriage, respect for property, truthfulness in public statements about other people and respect for parents (the fifth to the ninth commandments). These are also contained in the Sharīʿa, even though the form of marriage is different. Variations in detail may perhaps be ascribed to differences in cultural environment. There is also some similarity between the two religions with regard to the moral ideal for individuals, that is, those matters covered by God's command which are not suitable for enforcement by courts. In both religions, of course, there is a wide range of moral ideals, since those of the ordinary believer can be very different from those of the Muslim ṣūfī or Christian monk. Christians would agree with Muslims that these matters are based on God's commands or prescriptions, which cannot be changed. Christians, however, would be readier to admit that the application of God's prescriptions may vary if there are great changes in circumstances. In this they would place some reliance on sound human reason, and would also insist that experience must be taken into account; for example, a new law as formulated may seem excellent, but in practice may prove to have unforeseen and unwanted consequences; a law designed to give tenants of houses greater security of tenure may make landlords stop letting houses (instead selling them) and thus be to the disadvantage of potential tenants.

In the world of today there have been extensive changes owing to the growth of science and technology. The important question for believers is whether these have affected human beings to such an extent that there have to be significant changes in moral ideals and the laws based on them. One of the great changes in circumstances is the increase in the ease and speed of communications, both in the spreading of news and in actual travelling. What is done in one small town may be known all over the world in an hour or two. The availability of transport makes it possible to have vast conurbations of people and also leads to great movements of population, including refugees from oppressive governments. At a conference in Delhi on law and morality the Indian ulema present had their attention called to the plight of women whose husbands had disappeared and who could not obtain a divorce. Presumably in medieval times it would have been most unusual for a man to disappear completely but with modern communications it is easy; though a change in the application of the law on this point would seem appropriate and desirable, the Indian ulema were unwilling to recommend any change. This is a relatively trivial matter, for the technological changes also affect the application of the laws in more serious respects. From those who believe in an unchanging divine law, whether Muslims or Christians, a great intellectual effort is required in order to show how that law can be adapted to contemporary conditions and yet maintain its fundamental principles.

Secondly, much thought has to be given to the formulating of moral rules and ideals to be observed in the relations between states and nations. In medieval times both Muslim and Christian thinkers paid some attention to this field, and wrote, for example, about how a good Muslim ruler would act and about what constituted a 'just war'. In the last century or so some good practices have been widely adopted, but states do not always follow these; and some often follow bad practices. Something has been achieved by the creation, first of the League of Nations, and then of the United Nations. but much remains to be done to establish rules for the conduct of international affairs, and then to get states and rulers to obey these rules. A closely related field is that of the relations between the government of a country and its subjects. To this field is relevant the work that has been done on human rights; but here again much remains to be done.

Thirdly—and perhaps most important—is the consideration of the character of the authority possessed by such rules as may be formulated in the two areas just described, assuming this has been done in accordance with the fundamental principles of God's law. At this point difficulties arise because of the differing experience of Islam and Christianity. Yet some points may be made. Even if it is accepted that the commands are God's commands, it is proper to ask whether human beings have correctly understood the fundamental principles implicit in them. One of the Ten Commandments is 'you shall not kill', and this may be said to inculcate the fundamental principle of 'respect for life'. What may be asked, however, is whether this command forbids the judicial execution of criminals. For nearly twenty centuries most Christians have agreed that it does not; but that appears to be a human interpretation of the command. In the present century many Christians doubt whether execution is a good way to deal with murderers, and think that the principle of respect for life demands some other form of punishment.

When it comes to the detailed elaboration of God's commands, taking account of human experience, a basic question is whether a rule is to be accepted merely because it is satisfactory in practice and has good 'fruits', or whether human beings have something like a conscience or moral sense to tell them what is good and what is bad. Even if something like conscience is admitted to exist, there is the further question whether it merely reflects the beliefs and attitudes of the society by a process of, say, 'introjection', or whether, though it may be influenced by society, it is ultimately independent of it. This shows that, even when it is agreed that the commands are God's commands, there are still difficulties to overcome.

To attempt to deal adequately with these three areas would require a whole book at least. All that has been possible here is to indicate that, though there are important differences between Islam and Christianity about the manner of applying God's law to human relationships, there are also common features which could be made the basis of co-operation.

Chapter 5

God the Creator

Christianity and Islam agree that God, who is transcendent, is the creator and sustainer of the universe; but it is not easy to see how this is to be understood in the light of what we now know about the universe. The present chapter attempts to deal with this difficulty.

I Revelation and knowledge of the world

Revelation, it has been insisted above, is primarily about the mutual relations of God and human beings. In speaking about these matters, however, it inevitably makes statements about the relation of God to the world, and such statements are bound to be in terms of the human ideas about the world current at the time of the revelation. In respect of knowledge of the world, however, from time to time advances are made through the use of human reason. In the ages following important advances the believer in God is under some pressure to bring the assertions in his scriptures into accord with the contemporary conception of the world. This procedure has occurred frequently in the course of history. Two outstanding instances may be mentioned here by way of illustration, one Muslim and one Christian.

The Muslim is al-Ghazālī (1058-1111), who lived at a time when in the Islamic world Greek philosophy and science were becoming known to an increasingly numerous band of scholars, who may be referred to as the Falāsifa. The outstanding figure up to this time had been Ibn-Sīnā or Avicenna (d. 1037). The Falāsifa received their instruction in colleges specializing in the 'foreign sciences' and wholly distinct from the Islamic colleges where Islamic jurisprudence and other Islamic subjects were taught. The men from the two sets of institutions rarely mixed, but the religious scholars could not altogether avoid some knowledge of the teaching of the Falāsifa, and a few were a little perturbed by it, because they realized that they had no satisfactory replies to some of the arguments of the Falāsifa against themselves. Al-Ghazālī was so troubled by this matter that on his appointment at the age of 33 to the main professorship in the Niẓāmiyya college in Baghdad he decided to spend his free time for a year or two in gaining a thorough knowledge of the philosophy of Ibn-Sīnā. He was so successful in this that his book *The Aims (or Views) of the Philosophers* is held to give a clearer account of the philosophy of Ibn-Sīnā than do the latter's own works. He followed this up with *The Inconsistency of the Philosophers*, in which he listed and refuted the points in which he considered their metaphysical doctrine contrary to true Islam. In the course of his studies he also examined other disciplines, such as logic and mathematics, and noted to what extent they were neutral with regard to religious truth and so could properly be studied by Muslims. In particular he showed the advantages of Aristotelian logic in theological arguments, and by his writings secured its inclusion in the curriculum of Islamic learning. At the same time some Greek cosmological ideas were also accepted, such as the sphericity of the earth. As a result of al-Ghazālī's studies the contradictions were removed between revealed doctrine and contemporary human knowledge of the world.

Something similar was achieved by the Christian thinker, Thomas Aquinas (1225-74). Western Europe had recently become aware of the full range of Greek philosophy and science through translations from Arabic into Latin. These included both the works of Plato and Aristotle and those of the Falāsifa—the very men whose ideas had troubled al-Ghazālī. The latter's *Aims of the Philosophers* was among the translations, but, because the introduction was omitted, it was supposed to express his own views. Also influential were the writings of a later thinker, Ibn-Rushd or Averroes (1126-98). Where Ibn-Sīnā had been bascially a Neoplatonist, Ibn-Rushd was more of an Aristotelian, and the Western Europeans were fascinated by Aristotelianism. At an early age Thomas Aquinas came to hold that he had a dual vocation, namely, to evangelical perfection (as a monk) and to the study of Aristotle; and these two vocations could be combined in the Dominican order. As a result of his scholarly labours he produced one of the greatest intellectual systems the world has seen, in which he effected a complete fusion between Christian doctrine and Aristotelian philosophy and science. In this achievement he owed much to his Islamic predecessors, for even the Falāsifa had been at least nominal Muslims.

In the centuries after Thomas Aquinas human knowledge of the world began to expand ever more rapidly. A great jolt was given to accepted ideas by the theory of Copernicus and Galileo that the earth was not motionless but moved round the sun. In the early nineteenth century geological studies made it virtually certain that the earth was much older than the period of about 6000 years derived from biblical chronology. The greatest shock of all, however, came from Darwin's theory that the human race is descended from 'lower' forms of life. There was great popular and clerical resistance to these scientific theories because they seemed to be attacking important general ideas, such as the central position of our planet in the universe and the great superiority of human beings to all animals. Despite all the various forms of resistance, however, the scientific view of the world is now generally accepted by educated persons in the West. The position adopted in this book is that the assured results of science are to be accepted. In particular, this means acceptance of the *fact* of evolution, namely, that *Homo sapiens* is descended from 'lower' forms of life, but it does not require acceptance of any particular theory of *how* evolution comes about. This is worth mentioning because some fundamentalist Christians and Muslims make scientific disagreements about the mechanics of evolution a ground for rejecting the fact.

The present age differs from those of Al-Ghazālī and Thomas Aquinas in that there is no dominant or even emergent philosophy capable of going beyond the detailed results of science and presenting a comprehensive cosmology. Yet such a cosmology is needed by believers in God if they are to bring religious doctrine into harmony with our human knowledge of the world. Accordingly an attempt will be made in the next section to provide the rudiments of a philosophical cosmology by drawing on ideas from such thinkers as Michael Polanyi and Pierre Teilhard de Chardin.[1] This may seem to divert attention from the meeting of Islam and Christianity, but it seems to be necessary if sense is to be made of Muslim and Christian belief in God.

II A provisional philosophical cosmology

(a) The hierarchical structure of the universe

The conception of a hierarchy of entities with higher and lower levels, as developed by Michael Polanyi, has already been mentioned (p.39). The conception could indeed be extended beyond the use he makes of it. At the lowest levels one would have: electrons and other subatomic entities; atoms; and molecules. Above these in the purely physical world one might perhaps place: material bodies; celestial bodies (such as meteorites, moons, planets and stars); galaxies; and finally the universe as a whole. In the sphere of life, however, a different hierarchy would appear: mega-molecules; cells; organisms; human beings (in so far as they dominate other organisms); human societies; humanity as a whole. It is this last with which we are chiefly concerned.

The essential point about Polanyi's conception is that higher-level entities somehow impose boundary conditions on lower-level entities, so that the latter, while acting completely in accordance with their own nature, make possible, support and contribute to the activity of the higher-level entities. Polanyi applies this conception only to living beings, but there seems to be no reason why it should not also apply in the sphere of pre-life. The chemical compounding which produces common salt might be said to set boundary conditions for the atoms of sodium and chlorine included in the molecule of salt. Something like this would seem to be implicit in Teilhard's approach. Undoubtedly, however, the crux for this conception of hierarchies is the transition from pre-life to life. Polanyi insists that 'a boundary condition is always extraneous to the process which it delimits', and thus the 'set of boundary conditions' which constitute 'the structure of living things' is 'extraneous to the laws of physics and chemistry'.[2]

The case of human beings differs again from that of organisms owing to the presence of consciousness or the element of meaning. Consciousness directs the biological activities of the human organism with which it is associated towards the realization of the meanings which it has adopted. To be more precise, this is not just consciousness as awareness of objects, but consciousness as aware of itself being aware of objects. Consciousness is thus the 'within' or inner aspect of human life. Teilhard postulates a 'within' for all entities, but there is a leap forward from the other 'withins' to the human 'within'—a leap comparable to several others in the cosmic process. Nevertheless it is still true that the human consciousness sets the boundary conditions for the various organs and other lower-level entities which go to constitute the human being. These entities all behave in accordance with their proper nature; yet, when they are functioning in a healthy manner, they are subordinate to the realization of his purposes or meanings.

Though consciousness has the primary role in mature and meaningful human activity, an individual is usually unaware of most of the controlling operations taking place in the lower levels of the hierarchy which is himself. Thus he is unaware of the heart's activity in circulating the blood and of the metabolism achieved by the stomach, not to mention the activities of single cells and those of still lower entities. It is only after scientific or philosophical study that he realizes how much has been going on 'in' him of which he is unaware. Moreover, apart from the lower-level controlling factors of which he is unaware, there are other ways in which his consciousness may have incomplete control of his activities. This may happen, for example, when he is suffering from a neurotic disturbance or when he has imperfect knowledge of the circumstances in which he is acting.

The healthier a person is, both mentally and physically, the fuller the control he exercises over his activity. It has also to be noted, however, that there are circumstances in which his control of his activity can be seriously impaired or break down completely, for example, when he is ill or when he has been wounded or poisoned. When such things happen, the human organism may break down completely and die. Death is thus a failure of the controlling centre to retain control. In other words, despite the existence of the hierarchical structure, the higher-level entities do not necessarily always control the lower-level entities. The analogy of a garden is perhaps helpful here. The human gardener attempts to impose his meanings on lower-level entities—the soil and the plants. So long as he has proper implements, adequate time to work in the garden (according to its size) and propitious weather, the garden will more or less realize his meanings, though there will probably always be some aspect of it which might have been better. If the weather is bad or his time is too short, the plants he wants will not mature properly, and the weeds will begin to take over. With prolonged neglect the garden will lose nearly all the human meanings it once had.

In the list given above of entities found in hierarchical structures it was suggested that there were two types of entity at a higher level than the human individual, namely, societies and the whole of humanity.

Some people would deny this and say that above the individual there is no entity of the type with which we are concerned. Neither a particular society nor humanity as a whole, they would say, has a unitary focus comparable to consciousness in the individual. On the other hand, it can be maintained that there are some grounds for thinking that societies stand in a relation to their members not unlike that of a human being to his organs. By 'society' here is primarily meant something like Western Christendom in medieval times or like the community of Muslims about 1800, before it had been seriously disturbed by the West; but what is said will apply *mutatis mutandis* to many other types of society. Though a society does not have a unitary consciousness, it has other features of a high-level entity. Since the reality within which a person acts is a socially constructed reality, the society sets the boundary conditions within which he leads his life. Within these boundary conditions he lives in accordance with his own nature and tries, as far as in in his power, to 'do his own thing'; but since persons cannot be persons except through and in a society, they cannot act except in accordance with the meanings implicit in the world-view of the society. Thus there is a sense in which the society is realizing its meanings through the activity of its members. A society is not static, of course, nor is its view of reality; and it is always possible for the latter to be modified by the actions of some of its members. On the whole, however, such modifications happen only slowly.

In a discussion of the unitary character of a society it is worth reminding ourselves that there are ways in which a man falls short of being a perfect unity or of being fully integrated. At the biological level he functions as an organism, that is, as a single unit; but at the psychological level things may be different. Most human beings are not so divided as Dr Jekyll and Mr Hyde, but it is generally agreed that all have to work at what the Jungians call their 'individuation'. The aim of individuation is that a person should have awareness of all the different aspects of his personality, pleasant and unpleasant, and should be able to control his activity so that he realizes the meanings he consciously accepts and wants to realize. Similarly, it should be possible to allow that the unity of a society is something which is in process of being achieved, but which is not yet fully present. Sometimes a society is the sole occupant of a geographical area, and has a basis of unity comparable to the body in the case of an individual. This may make the integration of the society easier, as also may common physical descent or a common racial type, distinct from that of other societies.

To be a full unity a society must be genuinely integrated. That means that it must have a common system of values, attitudes and interpretations of the world around it in which it lives–in short, a religious world-view; and this world-view must be accepted by all the members of the society. The genuine integration of a society, however, must be distinguished from a totalitarian unification of the society. In the case of the latter people are forced into a common mould by use of the media and all the other forms of the modern technology of psychological and intellectual regimentation. In a genuinely integrated society, on the other hand, each member is expected and encouraged to develop freely his own individuality within the framework provided by the society.

Finally there seems to be no reason why humanity as a whole should not be regarded as a unity in process of being achieved. The Bible regards the human race as a unity through common descent from Adam and Eve, but in the story of the tower of Babel considers that this unity was destroyed through human pride. About two thousand years ago the Latin poet could write: *Homo sum; humani nihil a me alienum puto* ('I am human, and I regard nothing human as alien to me'); but it is possible that he was thinking primarily of civilized humanity and might have excluded 'barbarians'. In modern times, despite outbreaks of racialism, there is for the most part an agreement that the human race in all its many varieties constitutes a single species biologically. In our planet the unity of the race has a geographical basis. With the increasing movement of populations and the resultant marriages racial differences are beginning to be blurred. The incipient structures for the unity of the human race can be seen in such bodies as the United Nations and the various international religious communities, not to speak of international organizations for more restricted purposes. So far there is no one generally accepted world-view, even in the non-religious aspects, but with the great development of communications much of the secular Western world-view is bound to be universally accepted before long by all educated persons. Even the religions are certain to move nearer to one another as dialogue is forced upon them by the mixing of populations. Thus it may fairly be claimed that the human race is potentially a unity, and that this unity is in process of being realized.

(b) Evolution and its direction

The cosmic process is conceived in the world-view of Teilhard de Chardin as a single process, but there is a development from pre-life to life and then from life to consciousness. Teilhard took over the current conception of 'spheres', such as lithosphere, hydrosphere and atmosphere, and then, after the appearance of life, biosphere; and to these he added noosphere, which is where consciousness is found.[3] For present purposes it will be sufficient to combine the spheres in the area of pre-life as a single 'geosphere'. This means that within the cosmic process we distinguish the geosphere, the biosphere and the noosphere. To understand the nature of evolution, we must look at it with reference to each of these three spheres. As a working definition of evolution we may take the statement: 'Evolution is a theory which asserts that "the current state of a system is the result of a more or less continuous change from its original state".'[4]

According to the definition just given there is evolution in the geosphere. It may not begin with the simplest ingredients in the cosmic process and go on to the more complex; but it certainly looks as if, at least in the later parts of the pre-life phase, some of the ingredients are moving towards greater complexity as mega-molecules. It is this movement towards greater complexity which makes possible the emergence of life from pre-life at some point. In the sense just given the evolution of the geosphere continues even after the appearance of life and consciousness. According to some theories the universe could even experience a 'heat death', that is, a state in which the geosphere would be unable to support life. The question may also be asked whether there has been more than one transition from pre-life to life in the geosphere, and whether if life dies out (for example, by a nuclear holocaust), there might be a fresh appearance of life. According to Teilhard's theory there is no reason why this should not happen, though it is by no means certain that it would.

The conception of evolution most prominent in people's minds is, of course, evolution in the biosphere or biological evolution. It is here taken as an accepted scientific fact that all forms of life are descended from the simplest forms, and in particular that man is descended from the 'lower' animals. Whether a scientist may properly speak of biological evolution being directional and progressive is still debated by scientists; and there is still more debate about the means by which direction and progress appear to come about. It is indeed obvious that the course of evolution is not a steady and regular progression forwards. Sometimes circumstances change, and then species of animals and plants, such as the dinosaurs, fail to adapt themselves to the changed environment and die out. There is a sense in which biological evolution is still continuing, so that at some time in the future the species of *Homo sapiens* as we know it may have been replaced by a superior species of *Homo*. Another possibility is that, if a nuclear holocaust destroys mankind and all the higher animals, the evolutionary process will be resumed with the 'highest' surviving species, but will not necessarily follow the same route.

Before considering evolution in the noosphere, let us look more closely at the question of direction in biological evolution and how it may be brought about.

The common idea of biological evolution is of a process culminating in the appearance of man, that is, the development of the human species from lower forms of life. It is to be noted, however, that this idea is in need of some refinement. It does not imply that every species is continually changing into something higher. The lowest forms of life still found on our planet are probably the descendants of comparable organisms existing in palaeozoic times; in other words, many species have stood still for countless millions of years. It is even suggested that there has been some regression, where a species has become parasitic on other species; but this suggestion may be countered by asking if there is any essential difference between a flea and a carnivorous mammal. These considerations mean that direction and progress in evolution are to be looked for not in life as a whole but only in the appearance of new species which are in some sense 'higher' than existing species.

In this sense most biologists admit that there is direction in evolution. Even Jacques Monod, who believes that evolution has come about through 'pure chance', speaks of a 'direction' in which the pressure of natural selection is pushing human evolution; it favours the expansion of races better endowed with intelligence, imagination, will and ambition, and also of groups which are more cohesive and more aggressive.[5] Monod regards this direction as something which has come about accidentally, and so presumably not as 'progress'. Other biologists, however, such as Theodosius Dobzhansky, admit both direction and progress.[6] It is indeed difficult for a human being not to regard his species as the culmination of evolution, at least up to the present point in time. This can indeed be shown with apparent objectivity by applying various measures, 'whether . . . the morphological complexity, or the advancement of sense-organs, or of nervous systems, or brains'.[7] On the other hand, other measures could be employed, such as size; and then man would be inferior to the elephant and the whale. Perhaps the essential point is that the world is covered by a web of human meanings, into which the geosphere and the rest of the biosphere are taken up; and so to say that the human species is the climax of evolution is a reference to this fact and not simply a value-judgment.

The question of the direction of biological evolution is relevant to human living. A person urgently wants to know if he is part of a meaningful process. He can see a meaning beyond his individual life in the life of the community and perhaps in the life of humanity as a whole. But is there a meaning in biological evolution or, more generally, in the cosmic process as a whole? The matter will be touched on later, but for the moment we turn to a consideration of *how* biological evolution becomes directional. This involves highly technical questions, of course, and a layman in biology can only speak of it in a very general way.

Let us begin by looking at theories which may almost certainly be rejected. In the eighteenth century men were inclined to think of life or vitality as due to a vital principle which they regarded as an incorporeal agency.[8] This would have lent itself very easily to a theistic interpretation, but it has long since been discredited, and need not be further considered. Another theory, still advocated by Jacques Monod and closely associated with scientism, is that evolution has come about through the operation of natural selection on random mutations of the genotype. In the light of later experimental evidence such as that of C. H. Waddington, it would seem that this theory is much too simple for the complexity of the problem.

Waddington emphasizes what he calls 'the epigenetic paradigm' of which the 'central point is that natural selection does not operate directly on genotypes, but instead on phenotypes which are produced by epigenetic processes in which the environment as well as the genotype plays a part'.[9] In other words, when there is a change in the environment, a species of animals or plants will often adapt itself to the new environment in such a way that it becomes fitter to be selected for survival. Sometimes too a species will move to an environment to which it can adapt itself more easily, and will thus, as it were, choose the form of natural selection to which it will be exposed. If a species of animal chooses to escape from predators by flight, they will adapt themselves to this new life by becoming able to run faster; and those who adapt themselves best will be most likely to leave offspring. In the best adapted individuals it is almost certain that there is a genetic component which contributes to their success; and this genetic component will be favoured by natural selection. In this way the efforts of a species to maintain and propagate itself may have an effect on the evolutionary process.

In *The Phenomenon of Man* and in his later writings Teilhard de Chardin put foward a theory to explain the direction and progress observed in evolution. He postulated the existence of two forms of energy which he called 'tangential' and 'radial'. The former might be said to be energy as commonly understood; the latter, which could perhaps also be called 'centripetal' energy, is that 'which draws (the universe) towards ever greater complexity and centricity – in other words forwards'.[10] Both energies are present in all matter. It is radial energy which has led to the emergence of life from pre-life, and of consciousness from life. In later works Teilhard spoke of 'two drifts', which he identified with life and entropy respectively: 'the mysterious drift of the world towards states of progressively greater complexity and interiority, and that other drift (much more fully studied and better charted) which draws the same world towards states of progressively greater simplicity and exteriority'.[11]

Teilhard sometimes spoke of 'orthogenesis', but apparently used the term in an unusual sense. Its normal meaning is the unfolding of something already present in a rudimentary or embyronic form. This has been offered as an explanation of evolution, but most biologists now think it is not plausible. When Teilhard used the term, however, he seems to have meant no more than that evolution is progressive or, as he put it, that there is 'an ascent of life'.[12] In a late passage he defines orthogenesis as 'directed evolution' and maintains that there is not 'the least contradiction between the play of chance and the existence, in the object submitted to chance, of certain fundamental orientations or preferences'.[13] These orientations or preferences he had described in his 'Law of complexity/consciousness': 'Left long enough to itself, under the prolonged and universal play of chance, matter manifests the property of arranging itself in more and more complex groupings, and at the same time in ever-deepening layers of consciousness.'[14] Ultimately it would seem that what Teilhard is insisting on is that there is an 'orientation' in matter from the sub-atomic particles upwards.

In considering these rival theories and arguments a layman in biology must try to discern the points where there is widespread agreement.

One such is the centrality of natural selection. In some respects natural selection directs the course of evolution, since it is through natural selection that those species survive which are fittest to survive. To speak of the survival of the fittest is not just to say that those who survive survive. One can point to factors conducive to survival; for example, man may be said to survive because of his great ability to adapt himself to changes in the environment. Another important point is that living things have a tendency to act in ways which promote the survival of the individual and the species, including the numerical expansion of the species and the extension of control over the environment. For brevity this may be called a tendency to maintenance and expansion. This tendency could have been developed or at least strengthened by natural selection, since only organisms with this tendency would survive.

This still does not make clear what it is that gives direction to evolution. Natural selection must be accepted, but this is a sort of mechanism. It does not explain why organisms with maximal complexity/consciousness are fittest to survive. Perhaps this has to be accepted as a brute fact. It is clear that once organisms have developed the tendency to maintenance and expansion the epigenetic phenomena noticed by Waddington will lead to an upward movement. Ultimately, it would seem, something like what Teilhard called the 'orientation' of matter must underlie both the appearance of life and its tendency to maintenance and expansion. There is an advantage in speaking of 'orientation' because of its vagueness. 'Radial energy' was perhaps too precise, and Teilhard in his later years seems to have made less use of the concept. We are here dealing with something which lies beyond what can be observed by the methods hitherto employed by physics and chemistry, and an element of vagueness is an advantage. In essence Teilhard is saying that, since human life is what we know it to be, there must be 'something' in matter which has produced this. It is difficult to be more precise than this, but Teilhard sometimes speaks of a 'drift' or 'current' or 'orientation'. Such statements have the further implication that the stuff of the universe is favourable to the realization of human meanings.

The chief alternative view is that represented by Jacques Monod. In effect this view starts not from human life but from the current conception of matter, and what it says is: 'Since matter is what it is, human life *cannot* be what it is supposed to be.' The epistemological basis of this is the acceptance as ultimate of the current physico-chemical conception of matter. This conception, however, is fundamentally no more than a hypothesis put foward to explain the phenomena studied by physics and chemistry. It has, of course, been amply verified over a vast range of phenomena, so that many scientists have come to regard it as being of unquestioned truth. Yet in much the same way the Newtonian laws of motion explained a vast range of phenomena and were amply verified; but when fresh types of phenomena were taken into consideration, it was the Newtonian laws which had to be modified, not the phenomena declared illusory. Thus it would appear that, when full weight is given to our deep convictions about the reality of human meanings, it is not the meanings but the conception of matter which will have to be modified. This is the heart of Teilhard's thought in respect of matter.

We conclude, then, that the most likely explanation of the movement of evolution in a certain direction is that there is present (immanent?) in matter an 'orientation' towards complexity/consciousness.

(c) Evolution in the noosphere

Evolution in the noosphere, which is also the sphere of meaning, differs in some respects from biological evolution. One important difference is that, where the biologist deals with 'populations' (vast numbers of similar individuals), the student of the noosphere may have only one example of a society such as the Roman empire. This means that, instead of having statistical laws based on numerous instances, one may be dealing with a unique event which has been affected by abnormal or adventitious factors. Even if one finds the repetition of patterns in noospheric (that is, historical) events, as Arnold Toynbee thought he had done with his twenty or thirty examples of the species 'civilization', one cannot be certain that these are the causally important patterns. It is also difficult to know when a change is a change for the better; revolutions may have disadvantages as well as advantages. History certainly gives the impression that there have been more failures and 'dead ends' in noospheric than in biospheric evolution. This makes it difficult to be certain about the direction of such evolution and whether the cosmic process is moving towards some final consummation, be it Teilhard's Omega point or something else.

Teilhard speaks of the biosphere and noosphere as concentric with the geosphere, and also as above it in the way in which the atmosphere is above the lithosphere. This is a case up to a point with the biosphere, since most animals or plants live on the surface of the earth or lithosphere, but there are also burrowing animals and fish. The noosphere, too, is not physically above the biosphere but contained in it. On the other hand, humanity (the noosphere) is dependent on the biosphere, since we could not inhabit the geosphere if there were no animals and plants. Evolution in the noosphere is in some respects a continuation of that in the biosphere, but in other respects it is 'above' it in that consciousness is 'above' preconscious life. While it is convenient to use the terms biosphere and noosphere, it has to be realized that 'sphere' is here being applied – shall we say 'symbolically'? – to something which is not really a sphere.

In noospheric evolution, as in biospheric, natural selection may be said to operate, that is, it is the fittest societies or races which survive, but it is difficult to frame general theories about the factors which constitute fitness to survive. Evolutionary advance in societies usually comes from particular responses to particular challenges. Numerous examples of this were given by Arnold Toynbee in his *Study of History*. Adequate responses to a challenge develop new skills and new qualities of mind and character, and these may facilitate survival. The expansion of Islam in the century after Muḥammad and some of its subsequent successes is due in part to the human excellences developed by the Arabs in their response to the challenge of life in the desert. In the same way the present position in the world of Western Europeans and other Westerners has some basis in the way in which their ancestors responded to the challenge of the Atlantic and the challenge of the climate of northern lands which made farming more difficult than in the Mediterranean.

The skills and qualities developed in responding to a challenge are transmitted by education (formal and informal) to succeeding generations. In this process the world-view of the society, such as Islam or Christianity, also plays a part. The epigenetic paradigm of Waddington may likewise be relevant, and some slight modification of the genotype may occur; but more is almost certainly due to 'nurture' than to 'nature'.

Various tendencies may be observed in noospheric evolution such as growth in world population, increases in the size and numbers of cities, greater economic interdependence and even a measure of political integration into a world-system. This possibly shows a movement in the direction of a complex and differentiated, yet unified, society of all mankind. Teilhard accepted this conception, and called attention to the fact that the earth, and especially its habitable part, is limited in extent. As a result, when the human race expands numerically, individuals are brought into closer contact with one another, and this coalescence and convergence lead to a 'concentration of the energies of consciousness', and opens the way to 'a new domain of psychical expansion'.[15] The direction here is due to the 'orientation' present in matter, but it becomes more influential here than it had previously been.

III Scriptural accounts of creation

The biblical account of creation in Genesis 1 has had a great influence on the intellectual outlook of the West, but this influence may be due not so much to the biblical account itself as to philosophical interpretations of it. In particular it was interpreted in terms of the Aristotelian conception of the First Cause. This meant that people came to think of creation as the initiation of the Cosmic Process in a single act, and also as creation *ex nihilo*, 'out of nothing'. These are important conceptions, containing truth expressed symbolically, but they are not exactly what the Bible says:

> In the beginning God created the heaven and the earth. And the earth was without form, and void; and darkness was upon the face of the deep. And the spirit of God moved upon the face of the waters. And God said, Let there be light; and there was light (1.1-3).

This can be interpreted as creation *ex nihilo*, but the text is not fully explicit on the point, and the first word of creation is 'Let there be light.' The chapter certainly presents creation not as a single event but as a whole series of acts spread over six days; and plants and animals are said to be produced through the intermediacy of the earth, and fish through that of the waters.

More important than such niceties of interpretation is the fact that the Bible regards God's creative activity, or something very similar, as continuing indefinitely. The word for creation in Genesis 1, *bara*, is not much used except of the original creation, though there are a few examples, such as: 'create in me a clean heart, O God' (Psalm 51.10); 'the Lord that created you, O Jacob' (Isaiah 43.1); 'the Lord has created a new thing in the earth' (Jeremiah 31.22). The word 'create', however, is only a variant of 'make', and this and several other similar words are used in the Old Testament of God; for example: 'your hands have made me and fashioned me' (Psalm 119.73); 'you have forgotten God who formed you' (Deuteronomy 32.18). Apart from such use of specific words the Bible in countless passages presents God as controlling all natural and all historical events. Though wicked men are able to disobey him, he can, if he so decides, protect a just person from their attacks. This may be described as God's activity of sustaining the universe. In a sense it is different from the activity of creating or originating. Both sustaining and creating, however, have to be understood symbolically; and then there does not appear to be much difference in what they are conveying to us about the relation of God to the universe.

The Qur'ān has no long description of the creation of the world but only brief references. The longest of these is S.41.9-12; the others are all single verses.[16] Since these references occur in passages dealing with other matters, Muslims have not been so inclined as Christians to restrict creation to the origination of the world, though their theologians were familiar with the ideas of First Cause and creation *ex nihilo*. The Arabic word for creation, *khalaqa*, is freely used in the Qur'ān of contemporary happenings. One passage (23.12-14) mentions four stages of the embryo in the womb and says that God 'created' each out of the previous one. Even more striking is the repeated assertion made of God that 'when he decrees a thing, he merely says to it "Be" and it is'.[17] More generally, the Qur'ān emphasizes to a much greater extent than the Bible the fact that God constantly controls all mundane events, both natural and historical. Later Muslims made it an article of belief that 'what reaches you could not possibly have missed you, and what misses you could not possibly have reached you'.[18] Islam, too, paid much less attention than Christianity to the contrast between the originating of the world and its continuing control. For centuries an important school of theologians, the Ash'arites, adopted a form of atomism and maintained that there was a separate and distinct creation of the whole universe in every moment of time; this meant that, if a man shot an arrow at a mark in one moment, the arrow would not reach the mark unless in the following moments God separately created the successive stages of its flight.

There are thus differences of emphasis between Muslims and Christians when they think about God as creator and sustainer of the universe. The differences, however, appear to be mainly in emphasis, for the Muslim assertions have parallels in the Bible, both Old and New

Testaments. What follows is therefore based on the view that Muslims and Christians are essentially in agreement in their teaching about God as creator and as controller of natural events.

IV The cosmic process and the God of the scriptures

It is now time to consider how the scriptural assertions of the last section are to be brought into relation to the philosophical cosmology previously suggested. For the moment only control of the geosphere and biosphere will be discussed, that of the noosphere (or human history) being left to the next chapter. In setting out to deal with this problem it is worth noting that the scriptural assertions are kerygmatic, that is, they are joyful proclamations believed in with assurance, not tentative hypotheses like scientific theories. This means that our initial position is one of being committed to accepting their truth, and the present concern is thus only with questions of interpretation.

In essentials the provisional cosmology stated that the cosmic process is controlled by (a) the setting of boundary conditions, and (b) the presence in matter of an 'orientation', also spoken of as 'radial energy'. The suggestion that first springs to mind is that it is God who sets the boundary conditions, and that he is also somehow identified with the orientation in matter, or at least works through it. These terms, of course, are all symbolic, just as much as 'creator' or 'maker' and 'father'; and so apparent contrasts and contradictions may not indicate real differences.

The suggestion that it is God who sets the boundary conditions for the universe is in harmony with the assertions of scripture in that it places him above and transcending the cosmic process, and so controlling it. In Polanyi's conception, however, that which sets boundary conditions allows the lower-level wholes or unities to function in accordance with their specific natures, whereas the scriptures seem to assert that God sometimes interferes with natural laws. This difficulty will be discussed in the next section. A further difficulty, however, is whether we can be certain that these lesser wholes are amenable to the control of the setter of boundary conditions. It is indeed more or less implicit in Polanyi's conception that these wholes are so amenable, and yet the 'setter' has the appearance of being somehow extraneous to the wholes; it is as if they exist first, and then something from outside comes and tries to control them. At this point, therefore, the symbol of setting boundary conditions has to be balanced by that of the orientation present or immanent in matter. This is something which is found in all the entities in the cosmic process from the lowest levels to the highest. It is because the lower-level entities or lesser wholes have this orientation that they are amenable to having boundary conditions set for them. The boundary conditions might be described as the more explicit and external form of the implicit and internal orientation. As applied to God, this latter symbol expresses his immanence, the other his transcendence.

The question was left open above whether God *is* the orientation present in matter, or whether it is more correct to say that he works through it, as if it were some kind of demiurge. Those who are unhappy at the suggestion that God is somehow present in matter may be reminded that symbolic language usually presents only a limited truth, and that to attempt to find in it something beyond this limited truth is an improper procedure. To say that God is somehow immanent in matter must not be taken to imply that he does not at the same time transcend matter. God has both an aspect of transcendence and an aspect of immanence, and neither must be denied, even though we are not able to define the aspects precisely, any more than we are always able to state precisely the limits of the truth conveyed by a symbol.

To say that it is God who sets boundary conditions for the universe and who is present in the constituents of the universe as an orientation covers the main assertions of the scriptures. These speak of God's control of natural events in anthropomorphic terms; to say 'Let there be light' is suggestive of a great potentate of former days saying 'Let candles be brought'. The conception of setting boundary conditions is an attempt to make the manner of control more precise and more in accordance with contemporary ideas about cosmology, though it has to be admitted that it is also anthropomorphic, since Polanyi was thinking of an engineer making a machine. To say that God made or created everything implies his ability to control everything, so that there is nothing in the universe which has not a place in his purposes. To say that he created things out of nothing gives further emphasis to this point.

On the other hand, these modern conceptions do not give a very satisfactory account of the origin of the universe. About this, however, there are two points to be made. Firstly, the purpose of the scriptures is to give believers an understanding of their relationship to God, not to give a scientific account of the origin of the universe. Secondly, there is so far no definitive scientific theory of the origin of the universe. It has sometimes been suggested that the 'big bang' theory fits in well with the religious conception of creation; but on reflection it appears that the 'big bang' is more like interpretations of creation in terms of the Aristotelian First Cause than in terms of the opening verses of Genesis with 'darkness upon the face of the deep'. Ultimately the question of the origination of the universe seems to be religiously unimportant. Whatever scientists finally decide to be the earliest knowable stages of the cosmic process will be accepted by believers in God as an account of how God began the creation, for their chief concern is to assert his control of the process.

For the believer in God who accepts the assured results of science the scriptural statements about God's creation of man have to be interpreted in terms of biological evolution. Certainly God created man, but he brought him into existence by controlling the direction of the evolutionary process. God is not to be thought of as having had some kind of a blueprint of human nature; rather humanity is the highest example so far of that towards which the immanent orientation is tending. The details of the evolutionary process have been studied by Teilhard de Chardin in *The Phenomenon of Man*, and his account of this process may here be simply accepted.

The devout believer may well ask: How can I worship an orientation or a setter of boundary conditions? The question is a perfectly proper one, and the answer to it is simple. The believer must keep in mind what has already been said about 'sophisticated naivety'. By all means he may—indeed he must—go on using the familiar scriptural terms with naive simplicity. Somewhere, however, in a corner of his mind he has the knowledge that his use of these terms can be defended in a sophisticated fashion which takes account of contemporary science and philosophy. The attempt to express belief in God's creativity in terms of our provisional philosophical cosmology is made in order to satisfy the questioning mind, with which some of us, fortunately or unfortunately, are endowed; but when the questioner turns to worship he must put aside his questions and give himself fully to the familiar symbols.

V Problems in the interpretation of scripture

Even after the general views expressed in the last section are accepted, there are a number of problems about particular scriptural statements.

Many of these are concerned with happenings which God is alleged to have brought about in apparent breach of natural law as now understood by science. The first effort of the modern believer will be to try to discover what actually happened; but it is even more important in this scientific age to consider how the truth of revelation is to be understood and upheld.

(a) God as 'direct agent'

In both the Bible and the Qur'ān God is often spoken of as doing something, although the immediate agent is obviously some other being. The examples of this are very numerous. One of the most familiar seems to be accepted by Christians without difficulty; it is in the words of the Lord's Prayer, 'give us this day our daily bread', for this implies that the bread comes to us from God, although at the common-sense level it comes to us from the baker and the farmer. Somewhat similarly in Islam one of the names of God is ar-Razzāq, the Giver of Provision. In the Psalms there are frequent references to God giving victory in battle, although the victors had no doubt to fight hard. The Qur'ān (8.17) goes so far as to say that it was God who killed the pagans at Badr, though they fell to the swords or arrows of Muslim fighters. The Qur'ān also speaks of God as having 'made subject to you the ship to sail on the sea at his command' (14.32), although it was presumably men who invented the ship.

There is no serious problem in speaking about God as doing such things. Since he is the supreme controller of the cosmic process, he is the ultimate agent of all that happens, and so may be said to do everything. In normal English usage we tend to think of the immediate agent as the one who does the thing; but when we think of God as giving us bread, we are aware that he does so mediately through various natural and social processes and arrangements. What is to be noted, however, is that, when God is thus spoken of as apparently acting directly, although he is only the ultimate agent acting indirectly, it is only to be expected that there will *also* be a natural cause or a human agent.

(b) Alleged interference with the laws of nature

A much more difficult problem is presented by those cases where God apparently interferes with the normal operation of natural forces in order to help or to punish human beings. In some instances no important religious belief is involved. Thus when Joshua (10.12–14) called on the sun and moon to stand still in the sky and when they did so 'about a whole day', the modern believer will tend to assume that this did not really happen but that this was what it felt like to the participants in the battle. The religious message is that 'the Lord fought for Israel', but he presumably did so by enabling them to accomplish more in the available time. More baffling but less important is the account of the sign given to King Hezekiah of Judah to assure him that he would recover from an illness (2 Kings 20.8–11); in response to the prophet Isaiah's prayer God is said to have made the shadow on something like a sundial go backwards ten degrees or steps. That this should actually have happened is unthinkable, but there is no obvious naturalistic explanation, and the best course is to confess ignorance and accept the fact that somehow or other the prophet convinced the king that he would recover.

Of greater moment are the accounts of how certain peoples were punished for wicked behaviour. The flood which Noah survived was a punishment for the wickedness and violence of the inhabitants of the world (Genesis 6.5-13). The destruction of Sodom and Gomorrah was a punishment for those living in them, and Lot was saved because of his uprightness (Genesis 18.16–19.25). The plagues which afflicted the Egyptians and the drowning of Pharaoh and his army in the sea were partly to punish them and partly to gain deliverance for the Israelites (Exodus 5–14). Western scholars have used the term 'punishment stories' to cover the Qur'ānic accounts of the biblical stories just mentioned, as well as accounts of similar events in Arabia in which the tribes of 'Ād and Thamūd and other peoples were destroyed. A punishment of a less spectacular kind is the assertion by the prophet Haggai (1.5–11), that the bad harvests experienced by those who had returned to Jerusalem from exile were due to the fact that they had built fine houses for themselves and had not begun to rebuild God's house. This last example brings out clearly one of the difficulties felt by the modern believer. Bad harvests happen frequently in the course of nature, but why should this series of bad harvests be connected with the people's failure to rebuild the temple? Before considering the general question involved here it will be helpful to ask how far the other 'punishments' can be regarded as natural disasters.

Let us begin by looking at the Flood. Even if only the habitable part of the mountains mentioned in the Bible had been covered, that would have required several thousand feet of water, and is impossible. The most likely explanation of the story seems to be that a natural disaster, doubtless of unusual magnitude, has been further exaggerated by folk memory. In Iraq there are vast stretches of flat plain with a few gentle mounds, and an exceptionally bad flood could easily have covered an immense area to a depth sufficient to drown all living creatures —the text speaks of the 'mountains' (presumably only mounds) being submerged to a depth of 'fifteen cubits' (less than thirty feet). A somewhat similar explanation can be found for the story of how the Israelites went dry-shod through the Red Sea (or sea of reeds), while Pharaoh and his army were drowned. Along some of the possible routes from Egypt to Sinai there are great stretches of coastal sand, comparable to that at Mont St Michel in France where the tide goes out for several miles and is said to come in again at the speed of a galloping horse. If Moses had friends with local knowledge, he could have taken advantage of favourable winds and tides, while the Egyptians could have been caught. It is not being asserted here that this is precisely what happened, but only that this is the sort of thing which might well have happened, and that therefore there is no reason for holding that the bare physical events are breaches of natural law. Similar explanations can also be found for the other events described as punishments, so that they also fall within the course of nature.

If we may proceed, then, on the basis that the happenings by which God is said to punish men are natural happenings, how are we to suppose that they become punishments? As supreme controller of the cosmic process God may certainly be said to be the author of these happenings; but it is not easy to see how he brings them about at the appropriate time unless he interferes with the laws of nature. Yet acceptance of the assured results of science rules out the possibility of such interference with climatic and other natural forces. We are therefore brought back to the question raised by Haggai's interpretation of the bad harvests: how are they connected with the attitudes of the people addressed?

A clue to the solution of this problem may be found in a statement of the apostle Paul: 'We know that all things work together for good to those who love God' (Romans 8.28). This implies that it is God who makes things work together for good; and indeed that is probably the correct text and translation. This further implies that both good and bad happenings are turned to good for those who love God, and likewise are turned to evil for those who disobey him. In other words the bad harvests are bad for the returned exiles because their attitude to God was wrong, as shown by their neglect of worship. Noah's contemporaries were perhaps too obsessed with scheming for power to notice some obvious signs of danger and take precautions; and something similar could be true of the people of Sodom and various others.

This is still not entirely satisfactory. It does not explain why the people involved should have been punished at the particular time. During the ministry of Jesus a tower in Siloam collapsed and killed eighteen men. Some people thought this showed that they had been very wicked; but Jesus said that that was not so, but that the incident was a warning to all that, unless they repented, they also would perish. In other words, virtually all men fall short of fulfilling God's commands, and all will suffer in one way or another unless they amend their ways, though the suffering may be delayed. This further implies that the timing of the punishment is of secondary importance. If this point is now combined with the Pauline assertion, we get some such theory as the following. In the ordinary course of events people experience a succession of good and bad happenings. To those who love God the good are specially beneficial, and the bad do not seriously harm but may have positive or good consequences. On the other hand, for those opposed to God the bad happenings come as punishment and even the good do not necessarily have much beneficial effect.

It must also be emphasized that this does not come about solely because of the conscious subjective attitudes of those involved. Certainly love for God or opposition to him affect attitudes at a given moment, but over a period they also lead to the formation of good and bad traits of character, and these are objective in that they go beyond the consciousness of the individual. Some Christians would go still further than this and say that in those who love God there is an objective factor at work which they might call 'the grace of God' or 'the Holy Spirit'; and some Muslims would say much the same, though in different terms. In those opposed to God there could be an analogous but negative factor; to use a Muslim phrase, they experience God's 'abandonment' of them. There is much to be said for some such view of the existence of objective 'grace' and its opposite. Even apart from these, however, there are objective factors which, working through the succession of good and bad happenings, help those seeking God to a richly satisfying life with inner peace and bring those turning from God to a painful and unsatisfactory life. This is amply supported by the deepest experiences of many Christians and Muslims over the centuries.

At the same time it must be allowed that it is difficult for people with no comparable experience to accept such views. Both the Bible and the Qur'ān mention people who found it difficult to identify a particular natural happening with God's will or purpose. Gideon (in Judges 6.36-40) asked for a sign; he left a fleece of wool on the ground overnight and requested that it should be soaked with dew while the ground round it remained dry. This happened, but then Gideon seems to have thought that it might have come about naturally; so the following night his request was that the fleece should be dry and the ground wet. When this also happened, he was convinced that he had a sign from God. It is also recorded (1 Samuel 6.2-9) that the Philistines, when they thought they were suffering misfortunes from the presence of the Israelites' sacred ark in their towns, put it on a cart drawn by two cows; when the cows took a direction away from their calves and towards the Israelites, they regarded this a sign that the misfortunes were from God's ark. The Qur'ān speaks of people who refuse to believe that both affliction and good fortune come from God, when this is asserted by a prophet; one group is reported to have said 'our fathers experienced both dearth and wealth' (7.95), implying that this occurred in the natural course of events and was not directly from God. Despite this degree of scepticism the great body of believers continued to hold that natural disasters could be punishment from God; and in the sense just explained this remains true for us today.

(c) Adam and Eve

The story of Adam and Eve in Genesis and what is said about Adam and his wife in the Qur'ān cannot be fitted in at any stage of the evolutionary process, and the attempt to find ingenious theories to do this leads nowhere. The story, too, cannot be a historical memory, even greatly modified. It is best to regard it as a folk-myth whose purpose is to explain certain features of the world, and especially of the relations of humanity to God. Thus it implies the brotherhood of all human beings and their dependence on God. The Christian doctrine of 'the fall of man' is closely connected with the story and with the New

Testament interpretations of it, but it is also an attempt to explain the imperfections of human nature. The modern believer accepts the scriptural accounts with sophisticated naivety as containing in a picturesque symbolic form important truths about God. He will not look to the accounts for scientific information, but may find it convenient to use them to illustrate his own speculations about general human problems, including what is to be understood exactly by 'the fall of man'.

(d) The Virgin Birth of Jesus

The Virgin Birth of Jesus, or, more exactly, his virginal conception, is bound to have a place in dialogue between Christians and Muslims. Superficially they are in agreement, but this apparent agreement conceals important differences. It comes as a surprise to many Christians to learn that the Qur'ān teaches that Jesus was virginally conceived, but this is in fact so. In S. 19.16-23 it is reported that a being, usually identified with the angel Gabriel, appeared to Mary in the form of a handsome man; to calm her alarm

> he said, I am only the messenger of your Lord to give you a pure boy. She said, How shall I have a boy, when no man touched me and I was not wanton. He said, Thus [will it be]; your Lord said, It is easy for me, and [it is] that we may make him a sign for the people and a mercy from us; it is a thing decided. So she became pregnant with him, and withdrew with him to a far place; and the birth-pangs drove her to the trunk of a palm; she said, Would I had died before this and had been in oblivion forgotten . . .

This is not exactly the biblical story, and the rest of the passage is even less like that; yet the essential point is present. This further means that the manner of conception and birth does not in any way imply divinity, since many hundred millions of Muslims accept the Virgin Birth and deny the divinity. In their view it is a miracle like many others, that is, an interference by God with the ordinary laws of nature, and somewhat similar to the conception of John the Baptist by Elizabeth in old age (which is described in the verses—S. 19.1-15—preceding those quoted). For many Christians, the Virgin Birth, together with the whole Christmas story, has probably come to seem more central than it originally was; and Muslim beliefs will force these Christians to look more closely at their own. It is clear from the New Testament that the virginal conception played no part at all in the earliest Christian preaching. It is described in the infancy narratives in the First and Third Gospels, but is not referred to in the sermons in the Acts of the Apostles nor in the epistles of Saint Paul nor elsewhere in the New Testament. It is a story which came to be meaningful for Christians *after* they had come to believe in the divinity of Jesus *on other grounds*. Especially for simple-minded people the assertion that Jesus had no human father made it easier to think of him as son of a divine father.

The Christian who accepts the assured results of science has difficulty in knowing how to deal with the Virgin Birth. This position implies that there could have been no interference with natural processes. The fertilization of an ovum by some kind of divine sperm is also to be excluded. There remain two possibilities. It is possible that the story is an invention, and that Jesus was fathered in the usual way, probably by Joseph. It is also possible, or at least just conceivable, that this could have been a case of parthenogenesis, that is, the development of an ovum into a mature being without male fertilization. This is known to happen among some lower animals. If in very exceptional circumstances it had happened in the case of a human ovum, one could have expected a very exceptional person to be produced. For the modern believer the best course here is to hold that the evidence is insufficient to enable us to decide between these two possibilities, and that the infancy narratives are to be accepted with sophisticated naivety as containing symbolic truth. After all, the purpose of the Gospels is to give us, not factual mundane information but inspired truth about divine-human relationships.

(e) The Resurrection of Jesus

The problem for the scientifically minded Christian is whether in the resurrection of Jesus there was some interference with natural processes. Unlike the Virgin Birth, the resurrection of Jesus had from the first a central place in Christian teaching. The first task, however, is to evaluate the evidence.

It may first be noted that the contemporaries of Jesus believed that it was possible for dead people to be resuscitated. There were one or two Old Testament examples, and Jesus himself was held to have raised Lazarus and the widow of Nain's son. This means that the contemporaries would have been less critical of the evidence than a modern observer, and readier to make use of the model of resuscitation. Another point, however, was that the resurrection of Jesus was not mere resuscitation—to be followed by death at some later date—but was closely associated with his ascension into heaven to sit at the right hand of God, which is a symbolic happening. Yet the resurrection had also a physical side in that the body of Jesus disappeared. It may be taken as certain that neither the Christians nor their opponents, Jewish and Roman, knew of the whereabouts of the corpse of Jesus. The Christians could not have preached as they did had they known; and the opponents would have produced the body, had they been able, in order to refute Christian claims. It has been suggested that some thief stole the body and then left it to the vultures, but this is at best highly dubious.

Once again the best course for the modern Christian is to say that the evidence here is such that we cannot know what the physical events were but should accept the story with sophisticated naivety. There are certain points, however, which can be made. The first Christians had an experience of 'salvation' or 'new life', and this was associated with Jesus—with what he had meant to them during his ministry and with their conviction that he was still alive in heaven. At the same time this was not a purely subjective experience, but somehow or other had an objective basis. The objective aspect of these experiences—to anticipate later discussions—would appear to come in part from a transcendental or metahistorical or divine factor. The New Testament accounts of the 'resurrection appearances' and the assertion that Jesus is seated at the right hand of God[19] are the imaginal or perceptual form given to the experiences by the early Christians because of models pre-existing in their minds.[20]

(f) The miracles of Jesus

After what has just been said about 'alleged interference with the laws of nature' the miracles of Jesus present no special problems. In some cases what appear to be breaches of the laws must be regarded as natural happenings which have been transformed in the course of oral transmission; and there were some decades of this before the accounts were written down. In other cases it is likely that factors were present which have not so far been recognized and adequately studied by science. This last applies to most of the miracles of healing, since it is now widely accepted that somewhat similar instances of healing, inexplicable to medical science, still occur, whether at pilgrimage centres like Lourdes or through the influence of individuals endowed with healing powers.

With regard to other miracles, like feeding thousands of people with a few loaves,[21] or ending a storm with a word of command,[22] where it seems that the story has developed in the telling, it is to be noted that the events have also a deeper significance. The feeding of the multitudes is a sign that Jesus is 'the bread of life' (John 6.35), who is capable of satisfying man's spiritual hunger. The stilling of the storm is similarly a sign that he is able to bring peace to storm-tossed human hearts, individually and collectively. The presence of this deeper significance makes it even more difficult to know what actually happened. Was the feeding of the multitudes no more than a sacramental meal? Or did the sharing out of a few loaves and fish encourage people to share out what they had brought with them? Was it the fear in the disciples' hearts which Jesus calmed, so that the waves began to seem less threatening? Or, after he had restored their confidence did the storm die away naturally? The evidence is insufficient to provide an answer to these questions. It is relevant to note, however, that there was an Old Testament model for the miraculous feeding; the prophet Elisha fed a hundred men with twenty loaves and something was left over.[23]

For the Christian of today, surrounded by all the 'miracles' of science, it is more important to appreciate the positive teaching of the stories than to speculate about the original events or the extent of Jesus' physical powers. In the Fourth Gospel the miracles are explicitly called 'signs' (*sēmeia*), but it is probable that the other evangelists regarded them in much the same way. Jesus satisfies spiritual hunger and brings inner calm. Even the miracles of healing are not simply evidence of powers of physical healing, but may be seen as signs or symbols. Did not the Psalmist (103.3) think of God as 'healing all his [man's] diseases'?

Chapter 6

God as the lord of history

While both the Bible and the Qur'ān clearly express the view that God controls the events of history, or at least did so in the periods they describe, many people today find it difficult to believe that God still controls events or that he has in some sense a plan for the world. These are the matters to be looked at in this chapter.

I Sacral history in Christianity and Islam

The word 'history' is used in two senses. It may refer to the course of historical events, that is, events relevant to human meanings; and it is in this sense that we say God is lord of history. The other sense is more exactly named 'historiography', that is, the describing of the course of events. Any field of human activity or in which human beings are interested may have its history written; and some events may be written about in several different ways, according to the interests of the writer and of his potential readers. The essential work of the historian may be said to be to discover significant patterns in that great and complex chaos which is the course of events. The history found in the Bible and the Qur'ān may be called sacral history to distinguish it from most of the history written today, which is secular. The mark of sacral history is that God is active in the course of events, and indeed has a controlling influence.

In the Old Testament the sacral history of the people of Israel may be said to begin with God's call to Abraham to leave his homeland and go to Palestine. The story of Joseph shows how in a completely unexpected way they were saved from famine. Then God summoned Moses and strengthened him to undertake the deliverance of the

Israelites from the oppression they had come to suffer in Egypt. At Sinai he entered into a covenant relation with them, making them his 'chosen people'; and he subsequently enabled them to occupy Palestine and eventually to establish a kingdom under David. Later came the traumatic event of the exile to Babylon, which is presented in a divine perspective, as is the ensuing return from exile. The deutero-canonical books of the Maccabees tell of the successful struggle to preserve the identity of the 'chosen people' against the encroaching Greek culture.

The sacral history of the New Testament begins with the birth of Jesus through God's initiative, his preaching, his call to disciples and the themes of his teaching. Then a central place is given to accounts of his clash with the Jewish and Roman authorities, of his betrayal, seizure, crucifixion and resurrection. This is followed by an account of the early years of the Church and its experience of the Holy Spirit. The New Testament also contains some early Christian letters which are not part of the sacral history but which have a few historical details.

The Arabs up to the time of Muḥammad were much less interested in chronology than the writers of the Old Testament, and so it is not surprising that the sacral history of the Qur'ān is in the form of references to past and contemporary events in no particular order, and is not presented as a single linear history (though later Muslim scholars adopted the linear history of the Old Testament in respect of persons mentioned in the Qur'ān). The general teaching is that God sent a series of prophets in the past to various peoples, including Abraham, Moses and Jesus, and finally sent Muḥammad to the Arabs and to the human race as a whole. God also delivered Muḥammad and his followers from their enemies by victory in battle, as he had delivered previous prophets by various means.

For the Muslim, since his sacral history is based entirely on the Qur'ān, it is clear that the knowledge of God's actions in history is derived from divine revelation. Christians have not been in the habit of asking such a question, but, if they did, they would realize that the knowledge of God's actions is also mainly derived from his revelation to the prophets, including Moses and David. Besides the ascription of particular acts to God there is the question of his overall plan for humanity. In the Bible a special place is given to the Israelites as his 'chosen people', but in the later books of the Old Testament and in most of the New Testament it has become manifest that the plan envisages that the whole human race will be given the opportunity to worship and serve God. In the Qur'ān a special place is given to

Muḥammad as 'a mercy to the worlds' (21.107) and 'the seal of the prophets' (33.40), but it is also envisaged that the whole human race will be summoned to believe in God and his prophets. With regard to the future the Qur'ān seems to speak mainly of entry into heaven as 'the great success' (*al-fawz al-'aẓīm*). The Bible ends with the magnificent picture of the new Jerusalem (Revelation 21), which is primarily to be understood of the life of heaven, and yet has features which can be incorporated into an ideal terrestrial city and community.

II God's control of historical events

Sacral history presents the course of events in the historical process as controlled by God. One of the ways in which both Bible and Qur'ān claim that this comes about is through the direct action of God interfering with natural events; and in the last chapter an attempt was made to give positive value to this claim while holding that there was no overt interference with natural law. There are two other ways, however, in which it is claimed that God controls events: (1) he may initiate a series of events by 'calling' individuals to undertake some task or project, as he called Abraham, Moses and Muḥammad; (2) he may strengthen men to fight in battle and gain victory and to carry on in adverse circumstances, and conversely he may weaken the opponents of those he favours by causing them to lose confidence, to entertain false beliefs and the like.

With regard to the various experiences described as God's 'call' to individuals it will here be assumed that these, despite differences of imaginal form, are all of the same type, and they will be spoken of as 'inner promptings'. On the one hand they constitute an initiative by God; but on the other hand they do not destroy or override a man's freedom since it is for him to decide whether to respond to the call or not, whether to follow the prompting or not. Abraham was called to leave the land where he had hitherto been living and to go to Canaan where there would be a much brighter future for his descendants. Moses was called to return to Egypt where God's people were being oppressed and to lead them out of Egypt to the land promised to Abraham. Muḥammad was told he was the messenger of God who was to convey messages from God to his fellow-citizens of Mecca.

Two further points may be made about these inner promptings. Firstly, they have to be understood as due to the operation of God in man, perhaps through the intermediacy of angels (though this last belongs rather to the imaginal or perceptual form). In the terms used in this book they could be said to be due to the pressure within a man of the 'orientation' or 'radial energy', which is implanted in him by God and is constitutive of his nature. In Christian theology most of these promptings would be ascribed to the Holy Spirit. Secondly, these promptings do not come simply 'out of the blue', but are appropriate responses to the circumstances in which the man finds himself. Abraham was a pastoralist in Mesopotamia where the civilization of Sumer and Akkad had been very successful; but because of the precise form of its success it had apparently forfeited the possibility of developing further towards the ideal society based on a true knowledge of God. In the case of Moses, God's people was being oppressed in Egypt and threatened with genocide, and Moses himself was specially suited to be their deliverer from this situation because of his education in the wisdom of the Egyptians. Secular factors can also be traced in the background of Muḥammad's call to be the messenger of God, notably the social and intellectual malaise at Mecca as a result of the sudden change to mercantile prosperity from the harshness of desert life.

The second method of control is evidenced by many assertions in the Bible and the Qur'ān that God strengthens individuals. God's giving to men the strength, skill and fortitude required to win victory in battle is frequently mentioned in the Psalms (e.g. 18.39; 44.5; 144.1). Moses was strengthened and given the steadfastness of heart that was needed in order to bring God's people out of Egypt and to the borders of the promised land. In the New Testament the Holy Spirit is called the Comforter, that is, the Strengthener (though the Greek word has a slightly different connotation); and Paul prays to the Father 'that he would grant you [the Ephesians] . . . to be strengthened with might by his Spirit in the inner man' (Ephesians 3.16). In the Qur'ān, God 'strengthens with his succour whom he will' (3.13), and commands the angels to 'make steadfast those who believe' (8.12).

Just as God's people are strengthened, so their opponents are weakened. On one occasion God made an Aramaean army hear the noise of many horses and chariots, so that they supposed a great army had joined the king of Israel against them, and were filled with terror and fled for their lives (2 Kings 7.6f.). Even the Psalmist complains that God makes him and his people 'turn back from the enemy' (44.10). There is less of this negative aspect in the New Testament, but Paul, writing of believers in false gods, says that God gives them up to uncleanness, vile affections and a reprobate mind (Romans 1.24, 26, 28). In the Qur'ān there are many passages which speak of God setting a seal on men's hearts (so that they cannot accept the truth), or of his abandoning them or leading them astray. There is some discussion among Muslim scholars of how these passages are to be interpreted. Some think that God acts arbitrarily; but the more probable view would seem to be that God's acts of sealing and abandoning follow upon failures of the men in question in some way to acknowledge God and to accept his prophets.

The various methods of control are all found in one of the central events of the Old Testament, the exodus, that is, the escape of the Israelites from Egypt and their long journey to the land promised to Abraham. The plagues which afflicted the Egyptians were disasters which could come about naturally, even if not frequently. It was not the plagues themselves which brought about the exodus, but Moses' interpretation of them as signs of God's anger at the oppression of his people and Moses' ability to get the Egyptians to accept this (though doubtless they were predisposed to do so by some form of belief in divine activity in nature). Moses was clearly called to lead the exodus by an 'inner prompting' associated with the external image of the burning bush; and rousing the Israelites to leave Egypt and acting as their leader for forty years despite innumerable complaints certainly required divinely given strength and patience. In the light of all this it is perfectly proper to say that it was God who delivered his people from Egypt.

In the modern world men and women still receive inner promptings of varying degrees of importance. One of the most notable was that which led Pope John XXIII to summon the Second Vatican Council; but there are countless other instances less noticed by the world in general. There are also countless instances of men and women being strengthened to carry on in difficult circumstances. Sometimes, too, as occasionally happened in the Old Testament, waves of feeling can come over whole communities, so that they rush into a course of action which may be good or bad. An instance of a positive movement of this kind is the resurgence of Islam in most of the world at the present time; and there are also various partial revivals of Christianity. For an opposite example one might consider the possibility that God is allowing the human race to drift towards a nuclear holocaust because for the most part it has turned away from him.

III Sacral history and secular history

It will be useful at this point to consider more fully the relation of sacral history to secular history, since both may deal with the same events. All history is the discovery and presentation of significant patterns in the chaotic flux of events. The secular historian is chiefly concerned with those patterns which we describe as political, economic, social and intellectual factors, and the like, whereas sacral history deals with the patterns which are relevant to the Godward aspect of events. This difference of interest is important in considering the truth of sacral history (as will be done in section V).

The sacral history of Judaism, Christianity and Islam serves to define the identity of each of these religious communities; and similarly the secular history of a nation defines the identity of the national community, or at least may contribute to this. National identity, of course, is a feature of modern times. Though there were Israelite kingdoms from the time of Saul to the exile, their sense of identity came mainly from their sacral history. Something similar is true of the Islamic caliphate in its early centuries. The relation of Christianity to the Roman empire was different, but sacral history was important in Western Christendom from 800 to 1500. Modern authors have written what is essentially a secular history of the Israelite kingdoms, but this contributes little to any sense of identity. What it shows is how the historian's patterns of political, economic and other factors are applied in this particular case. This further indicates how Old Testament religion did not exist apart from the rest of life, but was interwoven with a series of commonplace historical events. At the same time it is made clear that, in order that the events may fit into the patterns of sacral history, they have been transmuted by folk-memory or otherwise transformed. When the secular historian makes use of material from the Old Testament, he has to take account of the possibility of such changes.

Another area in which the interweaving of religious and non-religious patterns may be observed is with regard to the inner promptings received by religious leaders. These do not come 'out of the blue', but are relevant to the existing situation in its various secular aspects, as has already been noted. This may now be looked at in more detail. It should be emphasized that the assertions to be made about the secular factors present in each situation have an element of conjecture in them and may need revision; but in that case something like them will prove to be true.

The situation in which Abraham received his call was somewhat as follows. In Mesopotamia an earlier period of desiccation had transformed the Sumerians from being food-gatherers to being cultivators, and the Babylonic civilization (to use Toynbee's term) which took over their technology also solved social and organizational problems. It seems probable, however, that this civilization, just because it had been so successful in establishing a political organization on the basis of irrigational agriculture in a plain, had become static in some respects and was preventing further development of human potential. It would be when Abraham experienced some specific dissatisfaction of this kind that he received the inner prompting to leave his country.

The case with Moses in Egypt was similar. After mastering the technology of cultivation by using the Nile flood the Egyptians had built up a high and apparently viable civilization with a strong political organization. Secular historians, however, have found signs of weakness. Toynbee saw the Pharaohs as having turned to self-aggrandisement (for example, by building pyramids) and to grinding the faces of the poor.[1] Another writer speaks of a 'psychosis for security', and of men coming to feel that 'the good life lay . . . in the surrender of personality to some greater force, with the recompense for surrender the security offered by that greater force'.[2] Whatever the precise truth about Egypt, it would seem that the possibilities of spiritual development were few. In addition the Israelites in Egypt had to face the threat of genocide, and this must have made it easier for them to accept Moses' leadership. His emergence as leader is doubtless due to his strength of character and to his education as an Egyptian prince (if the story is true). As an exile in Midian, too, he may have felt he was wasting his gifts. Both he and the Israelites doubtless knew the story of Abraham and believed that it was good to follow inner promptings and to seek spiritual ends rather than material comfort.

The appearance and growth of Christianity was also not fortuitous, but was linked with various external circumstances and with developments within the Jewish religion. Under the rule of the Hellenistic Seleucid dynasty in the second century BC the Jews were threatened with the loss of their distinctive religious identity through assimilation to the dominant Greek culture. They resisted this passionately both by revolting under the Maccabees and by developing religious practices which reduced contacts with non-Jews to a minimum. We see these practices continued by the Pharisees in the New Testament. By that time, however, Palestine was a province of the Roman empire, which did not try to enforce cultural assimilation, although many members of the Jewish ruling elite did, in fact, adopt Roman ways. Other Jewish groups, such as the Zealots, found alien rule intolerable and were looking for the chance to revolt; when the great revolt eventually came (66-70 AD), the Jews were severely defeated and suffered great losses. Even before this, however, it might have seemed to an observer that the true knowledge of God was in danger of being lost or corrupted.

At the same time there was widespread spiritual hunger. This is shown in Palestine by the great popular response to the preaching of John the Baptist and Jesus. The religious ideal of the Pharisees was making religious practice difficult for the ordinary people who in the course of earning a living could not avoid contacts with the Romans, especially when they were employed as soldiers and publicans (tax-collectors). In the Roman empire more generally the spiritual hunger is shown by the number of 'God-fearers' who were attracted to the worship of the Jewish synagogue but were not prepared to be circumcised and to carry out all the ritual and dietary prescriptions of the Torah. This was the situation in which John the Baptist and Jesus received the inner promptings which led to a revived belief in God and deeper knowledge of him, and to the spread of belief in God throughout the Roman empire.

Much the same is also true of the appearance and growth of Islam. It was at Mecca that Muḥammad first received inner promptings in the form of 'revelations'; and Mecca was experiencing social malaise as a result of the rapid economic change from a nomadic pastoralist economy to a prosperous mercantile one. While Islam had its beginnings at Mecca, it received a more definite shape at Medina, where there were also social tensions, perhaps due to the change from nomadism to agriculture. The expansion beyond Arabia became possible through the fact that the Byzantine and Persian empires were both exhausted after a long series of wars. The Arabs soon discovered that under the leadership of Muḥammad and his successors they were capable of defeating the Byzantines and Persians, and that in the existing power-vacuum they were able to move forward more or less as they pleased. Their aims were firstly the seizure of booty and secondly the acquisition of land, and there was no thought of making converts to Islam. It is important to realize that it was only the Islamic *state* that expanded by the sword, not the religion. The conversion of Christians and other non-Muslims to Islam came about by peaceful, mainly social, pressures after the conquered territories had become established provinces of the

Islamic empire.

This brief examination of the non-religious factors in the situations in which Judaism, Christianity and Islam began and developed will here be taken as typical of the paths followed by various human groups in their religious evolution. This leads to the topic of the next section, the possibility of a single sacral history for the whole world.

IV Towards a global sacral history

The sacral histories of Judaism, Christianity and Islam are from one point of view the basis of the identity of each of these religious communities, and therefore something which they cannot easily relinquish. Each community, however, when it contemplates the future, tends to have a vision in which it itself has expanded to include the whole human race. On the other hand, when the matter is approached from the standpoint of the world as a whole and when one tries to understand religious development as part of the total historical process, it seems unlikely that any of these sacral histories in its precise existing form is likely to become the sacral history of all humanity, although the major part of each, one hopes, would be incorporated into a global sacral history.

Near the heart of the difficulties in such a project is the view expressed in the Old Testament that God entered into a special covenant relationship with the Israelites, so that they became his chosen people. The usual interpretation of this, which has been widely held until the present century, is that God revealed himself to no other people. Christians in a sense inherited that covenant relationship and to it added a 'new covenant' (or testament), and so came to assume that there was no revelation of himself by God apart from the Bible. In the world of today, however, where there is much greater intermingling of adherents of different faiths, it is virtually impossible not to admit that God has been at work in other religions also. Thomas Merton, the American Trappist, found that the deeper his understanding of Christianity became the more he was able to appreciate the insights of contemplatives from among his Zen Buddhist and Hindu friends.[3] This makes it impossible to say that God chose the Israelites or Jews or Christians in the sense that he revealed himself to them *alone*. It is not impossible, however, to hold that he chose them for a special role in the religious development of the world, namely, to elaborate and present to others a particular conception of the ultimate conditions of human existence – that which we call monotheism. With this interpretation of 'chosen people' we can go on to say that God chose other peoples for other special roles, and that it was he who inspired the great men of India and China to make their contribution to the religious development of humanity.

Within the context of a global sacral history each religion would be seen as beginning with inner promptings from God to an individual or a series of individuals. Followers would be collected and a community gradually established. Life on the basis of the teachings of the religion would prove satisfactory, and the experience of the community over time would confirm and refine the teachings. Where the adherents of different religions were in contact or intermingled, there would be a struggle for existence and the 'fittest' would survive. In this way a few religions would develop into world-religions. The development would come about mainly through the means already described, namely, the giving of inner promptings, the strengthening of those closest to God's way and the encouraging of them to take advantage of favourable circumstances. The fact that the great world religions have lasted for centuries implies that they have made life satisfactory, or at least tolerable, for the great majority of their adherents.

In a global sacral history it would also be necessary to determine what important contributions each had made to the whole religious development of the world. Here one comes up against the difficulty that each religion has its own distinctive categories of thought. Thus while Jews, Christians and Muslims regard monotheism as an appropriate account of the ultimate conditions of human existence or of ultimate reality, Buddhists would not do so. As has been argued above, however, when one is dealing with symbolic language, an apparent contradiction does not necessarily mark a real contradiction. This makes it difficult, however, to find terms in which to express a global sacral history. Those used in this present discussion are inevitably Christian or at least monotheistic.

One of the claims made by Teilhard de Chardin was that 'during historic time the principal axis of anthropogenesis has passed through the West';[4] and there is certainly a sense in which the West in recent centuries has made the running in many fields of human activity, though there are some grounds for thinking that from about AD 900 to AD 1300 this axis swung away from the Christian West to the Islamic Middle East. If, however, anthropogenesis is understood as the process by which people become truly human, then religion plays a large part in it, as Teilhard would probably have admitted, except that he had little appreciation of non-Christian religions. More recent attitudes to the great religions, however, would suggest that there were other axes of anthropogenesis, at least in India and China, parallel to the Western or Christian axis.

Global sacral history might then be envisaged as beginning with relatively simple responses to a variety of situations. Some of these lines of response would converge with others and become assimilated to them, while others would fade out. After a time there would be a number of important religions, developing separately along parallel axes but with occasional phases of interaction. Eventually there came to be only a handful of great world religions and a number of minor ones. The great religions moved along parallel axes because each tended to exist in isolation in its own cultural region and to have few close contacts with the others. This state of affairs began to change in the nineteenth century, and the change has been even more rapid in the twentieth. Both aspects of communication – actual travelling and the spread of information–have been greatly speeded up and made easier, and one result has been a meeting of the world religions on an unprecedented scale. One result of this is that, where previous generations of Western students of Asian religions treated their subject as a purely academic matter, with books as the chief source material, their successors today usually have friends who are members of the religion they study and whom they meet as social equals. This leads to mutual respect and to dialogue, and after that no one can say what will happen. It is unlikely that the great religions will continue indefinitely to follow parallel axes, but, until the future condition of world religion is known, there can be no definitive global sacral history.

V The truth of sacral history

Finally we have to face the question of whether sacral history can be believed. Is it true? This question can be divided into three. Does God control the course of the historical process in the ways mentioned? Is sacral history true when it is different from secular history or conflicts with it? Does God will and control the general course of the historical process, and how are particular sacral histories related to this?

(a) The ways in which God controls the historical process

Three ways were discussed in which God appears to control the historical process. The first, found in both the Bible and the Qur'ān, consisted in the allegations that God has interfered with natural laws so as to produce events which were a punishment for evildoers and unbelievers and, less frequently, support and aid for believers. This matter was considered in the preceding chapter and it was argued that, although God cannot be said to interfere with the laws governing natural events, yet the total situation (including the characters of the human beings involved) may be such that certain events prove disastrous for unbelievers or, in other cases, advantageous for believers. Since God is ultimately behind everything, one is justified in saying that he has punished the unbelievers and helped the believers.

There are certain movements in human history which in some respects resemble natural movements. Among these might be reckoned the military expansion of the Assyrian and Babylonian empires. For the tiny Israelite kingdoms to oppose their great armies was like trying to stem the inrush of a vast flood. The capture of Samaria and Jerusalem thus resembled natural disasters, and the question could be asked: If the Israelites had not turned away from God and worshipped the Baals, would they have avoided the exile? To this hypothetical question there is no clear answer. It may be noted, however, that it was those of the exiles who remained faithful to God who triumphed over the disaster and returned to Jerusalem. This suggests that, had the Israelites previously been more faithful and yet had been taken into exile, they would presumably have coped with the disaster even better than they did. For example, after the fall of Jerusalem the governor Gedaliah might not have been murdered, and the remnant might not have fled in panic to Egypt (Jeremiah 40-43).

The second method of control was by 'inner promptings', including revelations to prophets. In many cases where those who received inner promptings followed them they were successful. Thus the effectiveness of the promptings was a matter of observation, and the only doubt was whether they came from God. The doubt is resolved by the fact that the divine origin of the promptings was a part of the revelation to the prophet, and so a part of what he asserted kerygmatically. Knowledge of the divine origin of the promptings did not come from observation of the external events nor from speculation about them; it is no way a hypothesis. Because the prophets and other men already believed in

God, they accepted the promptings as coming from him.

Because the inner promptings to Abraham, Moses, Jesus and Muḥammad led in the end to great positive achievements, it is easy to believe that they came from God. It appears, however, that there is little, if anything, to distinguish these inner promptings from others which did not lead to success or which were clearly mistaken. It is easy for a certain type of enthusiast to become so convinced of the truth of an idea which has come to him that he persuades others to follow him in wholly irrational projects. One thinks of the mass suicide of the Jones community in Guyana in 1978. The problem was known to the New Testament writers, though they expressed it in slightly different language: 'Do not believe every spirit, but test the spirits to see whether they are from God, because many false prophets have gone out into the world' (1 John 4.1). Even promptings from God, however, do not always have the expected result. Attention has already been called to the unexplained disappointment of the high hopes placed by the prophets Haggai and Zechariah in Zerubbabel. Yet sufficient has been said to justify the belief that this is one of the ways in which God controls the course of history.

The third way is the strengthening by God of the upright and the believers and the weakening of the evildoers and the unbelievers, both individually and collectively. Much the same can be said of this way as of the second way. There is evidence for it in the Bible and the Qur'ān, and the assertion that the strengthening or weakening came from God was first made by prophets. It is thus an acceptable assertion to those who already believe in God. Through later centuries many devout Muslims and Christians have held that they were strengthened in difficult circumstances by a power from beyond themselves, which they attributed to God. For those, then, who believe in God there is no reason for doubting that this is one of the ways in which he controls history.

(b) The details of sacral history

Doubts may also be felt about the truth of sacral history where it appears to conflict with secular history. Not all differences between the two are conflicts, of course, for the aims of sacral history are distinct from those of the secular historian. Sacral history is primarily concerned with the relations of man and God in the historical process; and there is no difficulty in allowing that alternative patterns exist within the flux of events. This would apply to the general picture presented by a particular sacral history, which may be seen as complementary to the picture given by secular history. When it comes to points of detail, however, the two histories may seem to be so far apart that they are not talking about the same events. Thus in the books of the Kings in the Old Testament almost all that is said about some kings is that they were pleasing or displeasing to God because of some aspect of their religious policy. A secular historian may mention the religious policy, but will also speak of the political and economic problems they had to face.

It is worth remarking at this stage of the discussion that the attitude towards secular history is not to be confused with that towards 'the assured results of the natural sciences'. Secular history may be said to have assured results in respect of establishing brute facts; but the main effort of the secular historian is in the interpretation of these facts, and this is done in terms of the value-system of those for whom he is writing. Since for the believer in God a value-system which omits the Godward aspect of human life is defective, there is a case for holding that the general picture of the historical process given by sacral history is superior to that given by secular history. On the other hand, where there is an approximation to 'assured results' in the application of historical methodology, the believer should accept these. This includes some of the textual and literary history of the scriptures.

After these observations we may look at two cases where there is a serious conflict between sacral history and secular. The New Testament has a story of how three 'wise men' or Magi came to worship the baby Jesus and offer gifts to him (Matthew 2.1-12). From the point of view of the secular historian it is almost certain that nothing resembling this ever happened. With this may be combined a passage in the Qur'ān (2.125-7) where Abraham and Ishmael are reported to have founded the sanctuary of the Ka'ba at Mecca. In this case the secular historian (assuming he allows the existence of an individual called Abraham) will claim that there are strong reasons for thinking that Abraham never visited Mecca, even though he cannot absolutely prove this.

To discuss this matter adequately let us introduce some general considerations. The term 'symbolic' has been used in this book to denote the non-primary use of words, but it is not so appropriate when one is dealing with stories or happenings. The word 'myth' suggests itself, but has unfortunate connotations of unreality. What is needed is a word that will indicate that a story is true, though only within certain understood limits. This kind of truth is found in diagrams, maps, plans and the like. The diagrammatic map of the London Underground with horizontal, vertical and diagonal straight lines shows with absolute truth the order of the stations on each line and the points at which one may change trains, but that is almost all. It does not show the distances between stations, the actual direction of the lines and the bends on them, or any of numerous other matters. Yet is shows with absolute truth what it is intended to show. The same is more or less the case with all maps. Many maps indicate heights by shades of green and brown, but the colours indicate only heights, not how the country will look from an aeroplane. In other words a map or diagram abstracts certain aspects from the total reality and shows these with complete accuracy, but shows nothing beyond these. This kind of truth will here be called 'iconic' truth, since it is convenient to have a relatively neutral term. (The icons of Orthodox Christians abstract from the full three-dimensional reality of persons and present them in two dimensions.[5])

We now say, then, that the biblical account of the Wise Men and the Qur'ānic account of the Abraham at Mecca have iconic truth. This means that they truly show abstracted aspects of the total historical context of the Christian and Islamic communities. This can to some extent be put into words. The story of the Wise Men has always been taken as showing that Gentiles or non-Jews also acknowledge Jesus as the Christ, while the visit of Abraham is an indication that Islam has deep roots in the biblical tradition, even though, as Muslims correctly assert, Abraham was neither a Jew nor a Christian. It is true that in the time of Jesus there were many Gentiles eagerly looking for a saviour, just as it is true that Islam appeared in a world deeply influenced by ideas from Judaism and Christianity; and these truths are presented in iconic fashion by the two accounts. It has further to be noted, however, that the two accounts are part of the respective scriptures, and that this gives them an objective character. This means that the believers are bound to accept them, but the acceptance may be with sophisticated naivety, as was suggested earlier, and in practice will consist in regarding the stories as having iconic truth.

The conception of iconic truth is not to be restricted to these cases of conflict between sacral and secular history. It applies to the accounts of Israelite kings which concentrate on whether they were pleasing to God or not, since such accounts abstract from the political and economic factors and yet add something to the (true) general picture of the historical context given by the sacral history. It might even be held that the truth of secular history is essentially iconic, since such history abstracts from the Godward aspect of events—an aspect which must not be neglected if individuals and states are to make a fully adequate response to the situations in which they find themselves.

(c) The general course of the historical process

The sacral histories of Judaism, Christianity and Islam assert or imply that God wills and controls the general course of events. This leads to problems, however, since there is divergence between the three sacral histories, and since they take no account of religions like Buddhism and Hinduism.

A consideration of these problems may begin by neglecting the divergences and looking at the assertion that God wills and controls the general course of the historical process. It seems clear that God has no blue-print of the process which he is carrying out in detail but that, by allowing a degree of autonomy to human beings, he has introduced an element of trial and error. This is similar to the element of trial and error in biological evolution. Communities have to try out certain courses to see whether they work. and this is so both for courses of action suggested by inner promptings and those coming from human imagination. Sometimes, even when those involved feel what they are doing has God's blessing (as in the case of Zerubbabel), their efforts may come to nothing. Yet on the whole there has been a movement in an upward or onward direction, and this is to be linked with the fact that God is the 'setter of boundary conditions' and has established an 'orientation' in individuals and communities. In this way it is true to say that God has willed the overall direction of the historical process. And it has already been argued that he controls the details of the process by giving inner promptings in suitable situations, and by strengthening and weakening people.

With regard to the divergences between religions, it is clear that the members of a religious community are more or less bound to accept its sacral history. Yet the present situation where religions are intermingling extensively leads to difficulties, and dialogue may lead people to modify, if not the verbal statements of their sacral history, at least some of their interpretations of these. Thus Judaism and Christianity would have to modify their interpretations of the covenant at Sinai and the new covenant of Christianity, so that they no longer imply that God has had no dealings with other religions. As already noted, however, the covenants may be reinterpreted to mean the conferring of a special role on the Israelites and then on the Christians; and this leaves open the possibility that God conferred different special roles on other religions. It is even possible to reinterpret the Christian assertion *extra ecclesiam nulla salus*, 'no salvation outside the church'.[6]

Such a process of reinterpretation makes it possible to envisage a global sacral history in which there is a place for all the great figures in the world religions. The precise form this ultimately takes depends on what happens to the religions in the future. As a result of the intermingling of religions in the modern world they are likely to come closer to one another in general outlook. A possible further stage is the recognition of one another as valid religions. Whether they go beyond that to become a single institution is by no means certain. Even at the stage of mutual recognition, however, some form of global sacral history might be possible, provided there was also agreement about the special role of each religion in the historical process. At the present juncture it is not profitable to go beyond such suggestions.

VI The end of history

Both Christianity and Islam teach that the historical process—that is, the world as we know it—comes to an end. This end is the Last Day or the Day of Judgment, and on it human beings are 'judged' in respect of their earthly lives and—on the simplest form of the teaching—assigned for eternity to either heaven or hell. The assertions of the Bible and the Qur'ān on these matters are relatively sober, as are also the assertions of the creeds; but in both religions popular imagination elaborated the teaching with a wealth of detail.

Attention was also paid to the period of history immediately before the Last Day. Jesus had taught that a time of great trouble was imminent but would be followed by the coming of the Son of Man 'in the clouds with great power and glory' (Mark 13.26; etc.). In the book of the Apocalypse (20.4-6) it is further stated that certain faithful followers of Jesus will live and reign with him for a thousand years of peace, during which the Devil will be bound. Finally the Devil will be overcome and destroyed. This is the origin of the beliefs in a messianic deliverer and a millennium, which gave hope to many oppressed peoples in later centuries.[7] Somewhat similar conceptions are found in Islam.

Their focus is the figure of the Dajjāl or anti-Christ,[8] whose period of power is usually no more than forty years. He is then overcome either by Jesus or by the Mahdī.

With regard to the Last Judgment itself the Qur'ān makes it clear that God and God alone is judge (1.4; 22.56f.; 40.20). In Christianity the official doctrine as expressed in the Nicene creed is that it is Jesus who will be the agent of the judgment, and this is confirmed by many verses of the New Testament, although in Hebrews 12.23 it is apparently God the Father who is judge. The passage Matthew 25.31-46, although in some respects it resembles a parable, is usually taken as a description of the Last Judgment; and the basis of the judgment is the performance of acts of mercy to the 'brothers' of the judge, or the failure to perform such acts. It is also asserted that those who do not publicly acknowledge their discipleship of Jesus will be disowned by him at his second coming (Matthew 10.32f.; etc.). Apart from this there is no clear Christian teaching about the basis of judgment, but the point is of minor importance in the light of the further Christian teaching about the forgiveness or remission of sins through Jesus (e.g. Romans 3.21-31).

The Qur'ān teaches that there is a written record of each man's acts of obedience and disobedience, and that this is produced at the judgment. There is also mention of balances, presumably to weigh the good acts against the bad acts (7.8f.; 21.47; 101.6-9). The judgment is passed on each individual as an individual, and God is not influenced by a man's wealth or powerful kinsmen (82.19; 44.41; etc.). There are indeed references to whole communities being condemned to hell because they were united in rejecting their messenger (10.28-30; 45.31-5; etc.). More and more the emphasis came to be on acceptance or rejection of the message conveyed by the messenger. In later centuries Islamic theologians held that no Muslim would go eternally to hell, provided he had not committed the sin of *shirk*, 'associating (other deities with God)'. This favourable treatment of Muslims is often connected with the doctrine that Muḥammad has a right of intercession (*shafā'a*) for the members of his community.[9]

The result of the judgment is normally taken to be the assignment of the individual either to heaven or to hell for eternity, but this is modified in Christianity by the doctrine of the atonement and in Islam by the doctrine of Muḥammad's intercession. In Catholic Christianity there is something like an intermediate condition in the conception of Purgatory; and some Muslim interpreters of the Qur'ān have found a similar doctrine there associated with the words *a'rāf* (7.46) and *barzakh*

(23.100). The delights of heaven and the torments of hell are described in greater detail in the Qur'ān than in the New Testament. Much has been made in the West of Qur'ānic references to the 'wide-eyed houris' who welcome the believers to heaven; but the Qur'ān also teaches that believing men, women and children will enter heaven as families (13.23; 40.8).

These are some of the main elements in the eschatological teaching of Christianity and Islam. Though there are also many other details, these do not raise any fresh questions and may be left aside here. Clearly this teaching is symbolically expressed, like nearly all religious teaching, and there are no grounds for thinking that it can be translated into non-symbolic language. What seems to be possible, however, is that it can be translated into more abstract symbols, and some contemporaries might feel these helpful. Thus it could be claimed that the houris symbolize the fact that in heaven men's deepest desires will be satisfied (and do so better than the Christian image of harp-playing), and also that a part of the satisfaction will consist in warm human relationships.

More fundamentally it can be claimed that the conception of life in heaven and hell lasting eternally is itself symbolic; that is to say, while the human mind can think only in terms of unending time, the reality is rather something which is beyond and transcending time. This formulation is still symbolic, however, even though it may be more abstract. It should also be obvious that it is impossible to say how religious eschatology is related to a possible 'heat death' of the universe. In the thought of Teilhard de Chardin it is noteworthy that it remains unclear whether the Omega point of which he talked is a consummation of the historical process or something beyond that process.

A more helpful line of symbolism is to consider how men are likely to feel if brought into the presence of God. Most devout and thoughtful Christians would probably realize that awareness of their sins would make them, at least at first, very uncomfortable. Only after they came to see their sins and faults as part of God's plan, and as forgiven by him and used for the furtherance of his purposes, would they find it tolerable to be in his presence. Conversely, those who were unaware of God's love and forgiveness would continue to be uncomfortable in his presence; and this might in fact be the essential torment of hell. Even saintly persons probably have not in this life fully entered into God's way of seeing their lives, and so still have to grow spiritually after death before they can feel comfortable in God's presence; and this may well be the truth underlying the doctrine of Purgatory.

Beliefs about the 'last things' are not an optional extra to Christian or Islamic faith, but express an important truth about the nature of human life in the present, namely, that there is an absolute difference between the life of the believer and the life of the unbeliever. Though the cruder accounts of the physical tortures of hell may be dismissed as merely picturesque, it does not follow that God is to be regarded as an easy-going, indulgent and undemanding father. Though he loves all men, it is possible for men to exclude themselves from his love and then to experience the torment of separation from him. This is an important part of the reality of the Judgment.

Chapter 7

Humanity in relation to God

Contemporary Christian views of the relation of humanity to God have been much influenced in recent centuries by the general philosophical outlook of the West, and so take a multitude of forms. It is therefore more satisfactory to begin by looking at the relatively coherent view presented by the Qur'ān and early Muslim theologians. It will then be found that there are many parallels with biblical conceptions, even though the latter are not prominent in contemporary Christian thought.

I The Islamic conception of the relation of humanity to God

The Qur'ānic conception of the relation of the human race to God is dominated by two words, *'abd* and *rabb*. In relation to God a human being is an *'abd* or 'slave', while God is the *rabb*, usually translated 'lord' but perhaps connoting rather something more august such as 'sovereign'. The service or worship of God is *'ibāda*, an abstract noun corresponding to *'abd*. This general conception further implied that there was a great gulf between humanity and divinity, so that the latter completely transcended the former and no created being resembled God.

The Qur'ān also accepted some of the beliefs of the pre-Islamic Arabs, such as the belief that a person's *ajal* or 'term', that is, date of death, was fixed. The pre-Islamic Arabs had ascribed this to 'time' (*dahr*) or 'the days', but the Qur'ān implied that it was God who had fixed the term and who had it written in a book. 'It is not for any person to die except by God's permission according to a fixed writing' (*kitāb mu'ajjal*) (3.145). 'God will not defer (the death of) any person when his term comes' (63.11). More generally, Muḥammad was told to say 'Nothing will befall us except what God has written for us' (9.51).

To those who criticized his decision to go out to fight against the Meccans at Uḥud he was told to say: 'If you had been in your houses, those for whom killing was written down would have sallied out to the places of their falling' (3.154).

Apart from such predetermination of events, there was also an element of divine constraint on human beings, as has already been noted in speaking of God's control of history. A person's faith or unbelief might depend on whether God had guided him or led him astray: 'if God wills to guide anyone, he enlarges his breast for Islam, but if he wills to lead him astray, he makes breast narrow and contracted as if he were climbing up into the sky' (6.125). Similarly, God might either help people or abandon them: 'if God helps you there is none to overcome you, but if he abandons you who will help you after him?' (3.160). As was also noted above, Muslim scholars argued about whether God's decisions were arbitrary or were based on the person's previous actions.

Although much in a person's life was thus predetermined, or at least partly beyond his control, he was thought of as essentially responsible for his actions. Human responsibility was emphasized by the sect of the Mu'tazilites about the ninth century. They insisted that human beings must be responsible for their actions, good and bad, since otherwise God would be unjust in condemning them to hell because of their sins. The Mu'tazilites were prepared to admit that it was God who on each occasion created in people the power (*qudra*) to act, but they held that this was the power to do either a particular act or its opposite, so that it was the individual himself and not God who determined which act was done, and so was responsible for it.

At the level of Kalām or philosophical theology the Mu'tazilites were opposed by the Ash'arites who are in some respects the most prominent representatives of Sunnite theology. The Ash'arite formula was that God creates human acts, while the agents 'acquire' or 'appropriate' them. This last conception, 'acquisition' or 'appropriation', came to be regarded as the most extreme example of theological subtlety. The Arabic word so translated is *kasb*, which was possibly used commercially for having something credited to one's account. The conception implied that an individual had a sufficient degree of responsibility for an act for it to be credited or debited to his account. In this way the justice of God's judgment was preserved. The Ash'arites also held that God created the act by creating in the individual the power to do the particular act. For power they tended to use not *qudra* like the Mu'tazilites but *istiṭā'a*, which might perhaps be rendered 'ability to obey'. They differed more seriously from the Mu'tazilites, however, by holding that this created power was a power to do only one particular act, not either an act or its opposite. To a modern Westerner this may seem mere theological hair-splitting, but the conceptions may become more comprehensible if he reflects that in willing each of our acts we presuppose that everything in the universe, and not least one's own body, will continue in accordance with its own natural law. and, since in the traditional Islamic view God is working in all natural processes, it is not too difficult to think of him as the creator of human acts.

In all this it is clear that in the Qur'ān and in early Muslim thinkers no use was made of the conception of human freedom. A person was regarded as somehow responsible for his acts (or at least most of them), but there was also a deep awareness of the constraints upon human action. Any idea of human freedom, however, would necessarily have implied a rebellion against the status of *'abd* or slave with regard to God. Thus freedom could be in no sense an ideal to be striven for, but only a disaster to be avoided. The chief way in which the modern Muslim rises above the status of slave is when he becomes God's agent or steward in this world. In the Qur'ān (2.30-3) there is an account of how God informed the angels that he was about to establish Adam as his *khalīfa* in the earth. The term *khalīfa* has as its basic meaning 'successor' or 'deputy', and was chosen as a title for the successors of Muḥammad as political heads of the Islamic state (anglicized as 'caliph'). The choice of title was probably not based on the Qur'ān, where the word occurs only twice in the singular, once of Adam and once of David (38.26). Because of the political implications early Muslim scholars found these verses difficult to interpret.[1] In recent centuries, however, Muslims in general have come to interpret the passage about Adam as implying that God has given humanity a position of stewardship in his world. In some respects this would seem to be an advance on the status of slave.

Finally it may be noted that the Qur'ānic conception of the human person is monistic in the sense that, where the distinction between soul and body was accepted, it was seen as only relative, and the body was regarded as being of the essence of the person just as much as the soul. The Arabic word which could be translated 'soul' is *nafs*, but in the Qur'ān it always, or nearly always, means 'self'. In the ninth century, however, translations began to be made of Greek philosophical works, and in these the word *nafs* is used to represent the Greek *psuchē*, 'soul', which is used in a dualistic sense, identifying the person with the soul to the exclusion of the body.

II Biblical views of the relation of humanity to God

Although the Islamic views just described seem strange to the Western Christian, there is much in the Bible which is parallel to them. When Abraham, Jacob, Moses, David and the prophets are referred to as 'servants of the Lord', the word for 'servant' is *'ebed*, which is the Hebrew equivalent of the Arabic *'abd* and is often represented in the Septuagint by the Greek *doulos*, 'slave'. In the New Testament Paul refers to himself as the *doulos* of God and of Jesus, and similar phrases are used of other apostles and other Christians. The reason why these words are translated 'servant' rather than 'slave' in English is doubtless that the translators were familiar with the Latin version and that the normal Latin word for 'slave' is *servus*. It may also be that by the early seventeenth century in Britain attitudes to slavery were changing, and that the word was coming to connote not the easy-going domestic slavery but something much harsher. Whatever the reasons for the use of the word 'servant' in English, it is clear that the Bible itself is much closer to the Qur'ān than appears superficially.

Some of the constraints on human activity described in the Qur'ān are also found in the Bible. God 'hardened the hearts' of Pharaoh and the Egyptians (Exodus 4-14). He strengthened the Israelites to win victory in battle (Psalms 44.4-7; etc.). He strengthened the prophet Jeremiah to stand firmly against fierce opposition like 'a fortified city, an iron pillar and a wall of bronze' (1.18). In the New Testament Christians are helped to do things by God's 'grace'. On the other hand, God may sometimes abandon, or apparently abandon, his people (Psalms 44.9). Mostly, however, the misfortunes and defeats of the Israelites are attributed to God's anger with them for forgetting him and worshipping other gods. In Exodus (20.5) in the second of the ten commandments God describes himself as 'a jealous God who visits the sins of the fathers on the children to the third and fourth generation of those who hate him'. In this connection there was a proverbial saying, which seems to have been widely believed, that 'the fathers have eaten sour grapes and the children's teeth have been set on edge' (Jeremiah 31.29f.; Ezekiel 18.2); but against this the prophets Jeremiah and Ezekiel asserted the doctrine of individual responsibility.

There are even traces in the Bible of the doctrine of predestination. According to recent commentators Psalm 139.16 teaches this doctrine, though in the Authorized Version it runs: 'in thy book all my members were written, which in continuance were fashioned, when as yet there was none of them'. It is now held that the 'fashioning' of the days is the determination of their number; and it is also possible that instead of 'members' (which does not represent any word in the text) one should understand 'actions'. In the Epistle of James (4.13-15), as was mentioned above (p. 54), the apostle warns those to whom he writes against being too confident about the future, and advises them to say: 'If the Lord will, we shall do so and so'; and 'if the Lord will' is exactly the phrase so frequently heard on Muslim lips, *in shā' Allāh*.

In the Old Testament the conception of freedom is apparently confined to the literal sense of freedom from slavery, though one also finds phrases such as 'you have loosed my bonds' (Psalms 16.6). In the New Testament, however, the conception is extended. Since the idea of slavery can be used metaphorically of slavery to sin (John 8.34), it is possible for Jesus to say: 'you shall know the truth, and the truth shall make you free' (v. 32). The same thought is also found in the writings of Paul; for example, when he says that if he does something he does not will to do, it is not he who does it but 'the sin living in me' (Romans 7.17), and when he speaks of people being 'set free from sin and enslaved to God' (6.22). This freedom, of course, is much more than the freedom of the will which is the basis of human responsibility. Apart from passages such as those mentioned in the last chapter which speak of divine constraints on human action and those about communal responsibility just mentioned, the Bible believes in individual human responsibility. At the same time the New Testament and later Christian theology insist that in general people are unable to save themselves from the condition of slavery to sin, however described.

In the New Testament the possibility is also presented of man rising above the status of slave to God, since it is repeatedly affirmed that the Christian believer has been raised to the status of 'son'. The essential distinction seems to be that the slave or servant does not know what the master is about, whereas the son does.[2] More will be said about this presently. In Christian thinking a closely associated conception is that each believer has a duty to exercise on behalf of God's purpose a stewardship of his talents, time and money.

Finally there is the question of the monistic and dualistic conceptions of the human being. The New Testament is on the whole monistic. Thus Jesus is reported to have said: 'if your hand offends you cut it off; it is better for you to enter into life maimed, than having two hands to go into hell' (Mark 9.43; Matthew 5.30); and this implies that the body shares in the life of heaven or hell, and so is of the essence of the person. Belief in the resurrection of the human body is also reflected in the Apostles' and Nicene Creeds, although the English of the latter, which speaks of the 'resurrection of the dead', conceals the fact that the Greek *nekrōn* properly means 'dead bodies'. As Christianity came to be influenced by Greek philosophical thought, however, Christians came to think very much in terms of Greek dualism, to distinguish the mortal body from the immortal soul, and to identify the latter with the person. An example of this dualistic thinking is found in one of the Anglican prayers for Compline, where the request is made that 'when our bodies lie in the dust, our souls may live with thee'.

III A contemporary interpretation of the scriptural conceptions

Modern believers, both Christians and Muslims, accept the basic formulations of their faiths as contained in scriptures and creeds, but they are not necessarily committed to accepting all the non-religious ideas found in these documents or held by their fellow-believers in later generations. In questions about the relation between humanity and God, however, both religious and non-religious matters are involved. The essence of the human being may be largely a non-religious matter, but what is held about it affects what is asserted about the relationship of humanity to God. To say what a human being is, or who 'I' am, is a complex and difficult matter, and philosophers from Plato onwards have produced countless theories. All that can be attempted here is to outline a view roughly compatible with the philosophical positions already adopted, and in its light to consider the scriptural assertions.

(a) Monistic and dualistic views of the human being

A human being was described above as a hierarchy of entities on higher and lower levels, all of which in some sense function as wholes but have boundary conditions set for them by the higher entities. Among the lower-level entities are the cells, each of which unifies and controls its chemical constituents, though without infringing their specific properties. At a higher level are limbs and organs. The summit of the hierarchy which is the human being is the 'I'. This is sometimes identified with consciousness, but the latter is not strictly an entity, but merely the 'I' being conscious or aware, just as the will is not a distinct entity but merely the 'I' willing or deciding. These two terms indicate two main aspects of the functioning of the 'I', namely, to be aware of the main features of the situational reality within which the human being has to act, and to direct this activity towards the realization of the meanings (ends) which the human being is pursuing. The reality within which action takes place has been 'socially constructed' as explained above. It is also to be noted that the 'I' is far from being fully aware of all the lower-level entities and their operations.

When the actions of a human being are in accordance with what the 'I' directed, the person is said to be acting 'freely' as this term is understood by common sense. Although the Old Testament and the Qur'ān do not speak of 'freedom' or 'freedom of will' in this sense, they regard such acts as acts of the person in question. Even those Muslim theologians who maximized the participation of God in human action still allowed that in an important sense the acts were the person's acts. Even common sense, of course, recognized various constraints on human freedom, such as when the warders forcibly thrust the criminal into a cell, and these constraints will presently be considered more fully.

The conception of a human being as a hierarchy of entities functioning as a whole is monistic. Although the 'I' can be distinguished from the lower-level entities, it functions only in the closest association with them. The action described by the words 'I planted a tree' is an action of the whole human being. It is also possible to make a distinction between the world of meaning and the material world, in which in appropriate conditions dead bodies moulder away or otherwise decay; but this distinction does not in itself justify a dualistic conception of the human being. In this connection it has to be remembered that the traditional Christian and Muslim view (based on a monistic conception) was that dead and mouldering bodies were somehow restored to life on the Last Day, possibly in a more glorious form.[3] The suggestion made in the previous chapter that a person's whole life-process may be raised into a sphere beyond time and space may be regarded as symbolically equivalent to the conception of the resurrection of the body.

The freedom of the human will is denied by scientism on the ground that what a human being does is determined by the physico-chemical constituents of his body. This argument, however, is now seen to be somewhat weak, since it fails to allow for the unified activity of the human being, in which the 'I' and other high-level entities control the lower-level (physico-chemical and other) entities without infringing their autonomous functioning. Even physico-chemical mechanisms of control and unification do not fully account for the activity of a human being as a single whole.

(b) Humanity's servile status or creatureliness

While the conception of the human being as God's *'abd* or slave has a central place in Islamic thinking, the modern Western Christian is not happy with the term 'slave'—perhaps because of the connotations of the word in Western society since the sixteenth century. Christians will speak of the themselves as 'God's servants' but hardly of their 'servile status'. Christians seem to prefer the term 'creatureliness' to express approximately the same conception.

One aspect of creatureliness or servile status is that human beings do not make themselves. Even their parents did not make them, strictly speaking, but only handed on the life which they themselves had received. Nor do human beings make their environment, even though each generation is capable of making relatively small changes in it. The environment on which our lives are dependent ultimately comes from God despite the fact that human beings have contributed to intermediate stages in its development.

Another aspect of creatureliness is seen in the constraints to which human activity is subject. Some of these are recognized by common sense. The most obvious is where physical force is used against someone. Apart from such external constraint there are various forms of internal constraint. Where a person has a distorted idea of some aspect of the reality in which he has to act, or is unaware of some important feature of it, it may be impossible for him to carry out the act he decided on, and, at least in some cases, he cannot be said to be acting freely.

Still more important are the constraints on human action not usually recognized by common sense. Among these is the unconscious neurotic impulse which leads someone to do something his 'I' did not deliberately will to do. This is perhaps partly recognized by common sense, since there is a famous passage in Paul's letter to the Romans (7.15-20) where he says that he finds himself doing sinful things he did not intend or want to do, and that in such cases it is not he who does these things but sin living in him. While Paul had thus become partly conscious of the internal struggle, the person acting on an unconscious neurotic impulse is wholly unaware of his motivation and thinks he is acting freely. Acts based on such impulses are often trivial and harmless, but sometimes they are socially undesirable and even dangerous. Since virtually none of us is fully aware of all the neurotic tendencies in his psyche, we are all in varying degree subject to this form of constraint.

We are also subject to what may be called social constraints. There are subtle forms of propaganda which not merely exercise constraint but even, in the view of Thomas Merton, do violence to the human being.[4] Such propaganda has every appearance of truth and reasonability and in this way 'predetermines us to certain conclusions, and does so in such a way that we imagine we are fully free in reaching them by our own judgement and our own thought'. Propaganda, of course, is consciously and deliberately created by someone. There are still subtler forms of social constraint, however, for which no individual or group is directly responsible. Constraint results from the phenomena to which the theory of the 'social construction of reality' drew attention (2.I(a) above). When I am aware of the realities of the world in which I have to act, I normally suppose that this awareness is the result of what I have been taught or have read or observed. I fail to realize that, even when I am relying on personal observation, I have, metaphorically speaking, been observing through spectacles which are almost certainly distorted in some respects. The spectacles are the view of reality which I have accepted from my cultural environment. Since I have 'internalized' it and made it mine, I am not aware of it exercising constraint; and yet it restricts the categories I may use in ordering what I observe, and the valuations I may place on actions and situations. In so far as the socially constructed view of reality is true, there is no problem; but the difficulty is that I am, as it were, shut up within this view of reality and so have no neutral vantage point from which to examine it and see how far it is true and how far false.

By way of illustrating this point we may look at one aspect of the life of Jesus, his attitude to the Sabbath. In general he was criticizing and challenging the socially constructed view of reality held by many classes within the Jewish society of the time. In this view great importance was attached to the keeping of the Sabbath, that is, doing no work in it. From the time of the exodus from Egypt the Sabbath had been a sign of the covenant-relationship between God and his people, the Israelites; and because of this to do work in it was to defile it and was punishable by death.[5] It is even recorded that a man was stoned to death for the apparently trivial offence of picking up a few sticks on the Sabbath;[6] the reason for such severity was doubtless that the man was felt to be jeopardizing the whole people's covenant relationship with God. In the case of Jesus, when he healed a man on the Sabbath, this was felt to be 'work' and so a defilement of the Sabbath. Jesus pointed out that it was common practice to lead an ox or ass to watering on the Sabbath (Luke 13.15). This implied that it was commonly held that, where the welfare of domestic animals was concerned, some 'work' was permissible on the Sabbath; and Jesus argued that the welfare of a human being was even stronger justification for allowing the 'work' involved in healing.

Those persons who attacked Jesus in this matter doubtless supposed that they were acting freely in defence of a religious principle. The observer, however, is able to see that the view of reality current in their social milieu had become distorted, in that undue importance was being attached to the keeping of the Sabbath while other equally or more important principles were being neglected. Jesus expressed this point when he spoke of 'the weightier matters of the Law, justice, mercy and good faith' (Matthew 23.23). This further suggests that there was a more fundamental distortion in the current view of reality, namely, the idea that there was great merit in the meticulous keeping of precisely formulated rules, and probably greater merit than in trying to come closer to the imprecise and never fully attainable ideals of virtuous conduct. This last distortion is also found in other religions and in other centuries.

Since it is a universal phenomenon that human beings live within the socially constructed view of reality into which they have grown, and cannot observe or think about that reality except in the terms provided by that view, there are numerous examples to illustrate the matter. Views of reality vary, however, in their degree of freedom from distortion; some are largely true at least in certain respects, while others are seriously distorted. It is sometimes difficult, too, to give a precise statement of the distortions. Everywhere, however, the view of reality people have accepted from their cultural milieu determines the form of their awareness of the world around them. The pagan Meccan opponents of Muḥammad could only understand what he was doing in terms of their pre-existing ideas; since they had no experience of revelation from God, some supposed that Muḥammad was *majnūn*, 'mad', 'possessed by jinn',[7] while others alleged that he had one or more human assistants.[8]

Another very pertinent example here is the distorted image of Islam elaborated by scholars in Western Christendom between the twelfth and fourteenth centuries.[9] Once the earlier scholars had sketched the outlines of the distorted image, later scholars on gaining further correct information from Arabic books were unable to accept it objectively but could only see it as a new facet of the distorted image. Even the earlier medieval scholars were probably influenced in part by ideas about Islam derived from folk-memory. This medieval image of Islam has continued to mould the thinking of Westerners into the present century, though new attitudes began to emerge about 1700 and something has been achieved in correcting the worst distortions.

While the personal and social constraints to which the human being is subject are marks of his 'creatureliness' or status of *'abd*, he is nevertheless capable of rejecting revealed messages and disobeying God's commands. In so doing he is responsible for his action, and God would be acting justly in punishing him. On this point Christianity and Islam are in agreement, and also in holding that human disobedience cannot thwart God's purposes, though Islam would perhaps place more emphasis on God's continuing control of events.

(c) Stewardship and sonship

It was seen above that the New Testament teaches that human beings may become 'sons' and 'daughters' of God and so rise above the status of slave or servant. It was also suggested that when Muslims apply to themselves generally the Qur'ānic account of how God made Adam his *khalīfa* on earth, this is raising them, at least slightly, above servile status, since one who acts for God as his 'agent' or 'steward' is more than a mere slave.

As is well known, the Qur'ān denies the possibility of God having sons and daughters (6.100; etc.), and this applies both to pagan beliefs and to Christian belief about Jesus. Presumably the Qur'ān made these assertions because many of Muḥammad's contemporaries understood these terms literally. It is noteworthy that the theologian ash-Shahrastānī (d. 1153), when discussing the Christian use of the term 'son of God', commented: 'perhaps that is a linguistic metaphor [*majāz al-lugha*], as when one says of the seekers of [this] world "sons of the world [*ad-dunya*]" and of the seekers of the world-to-come "sons of the world-to-come [*al-ākhira*]"'. Ash-Shahrastānī was well versed in philosophy and this made him see that Christian theologians discussing the three hypostases (*aqānīm*) of God, did not take 'son' in a literal sense but used philosophical conceptions not unlike those he himself employed.

For both Muslims and Christians discussing the Christian doctrine that Jesus is 'the son of God' or 'God the Son', it is important to understand the earlier history of this term. In the Old Testament there are a number of passages where it is applied to human beings. Thus in Hosea (1.10) after the Israelites have been restored to God's favour by his initiative, we are told: 'in the place where it was said to them, You are not my people, there it shall be said to them, You are the sons of the living God'. Another passage is Isaiah 43.6: (God says) 'I will say to the north . . . bring my sons from far, and my daughters from the ends of the earth'. Correspondingly, God is spoken of as 'father' (as in Isaiah 63.16; 64.8; Jeremiah 3.19). More specifically, the Messiah, the deliverer expected by the Jews, was sometimes spoken of as God's son and God as his father (Psalms 2.7; 89.26f.; 2 Samuel 7.14). In accordance with this we find in the New Testament that the Jews are reported as saying, 'We have one father, even God' (John 8.41).

In the New Testament it is important to note that there are many references to the belief that all Christians are 'children' of God, such as John 1.12f.: 'As many as received him, to them gave he power to become the children [*tekna*] of God, even to them that believe on his name, who were born, not of blood, nor of the will of the flesh, nor of the will of man, but of God.' 'Sons' is also used, and on one occasion 'daughters': 'I will receive you, and will be a father unto you, and you shall be my sons and daughters, says the Lord Almighty' (2 Corinthians 6.17f., with an inexact reference to Isaiah 43.6). Thus in a sense the problem becomes to state how the sonship of Jesus differs from that of his followers. One suggestion is that the followers are sons 'by adoption' (Galatians 4.5), another that he is 'eldest [*prōtotokos*] of many brothers' (Romans 8.29). These suggestions do not harmonize with one another, though this does not matter when we are dealing with symbolic language; but in any case they do not seem to have come into common use. Perhaps it will be easier to understand the relationship of the two sonships if we look at some of the hints given in the New Testament to fill out the conception.

There are a number of passages which speak of God as the master of a house. The most important is John 15.15: 'henceforth I do not call you slaves [servants], for the slave does not know what his lord does; but I have called you friends, for all that I have heard from my father, I have made known to you'. This implies that the slave or servant does not know what the plans and purposes of his master are whereas the son does ('son' is implied by 'father'), and shares this knowledge with his friends.[10] In particular Christians claim that Jesus had insight into the fact that evil can be overcome by acceptance of the suffering it brings in a spirit of love. Thus it could be said that all Christians share the sonship of Jesus in so far as they come to understand this principle of the overcoming of evil by the acceptance of suffering in love.

In the light of what was said earlier about symbolic language, the conception of 'son of God' is to be regarded as expressing, in the best way possible for us, something real about God. The symbol of divine sonship implies that a human being may have insight into his purposes and into his relationship with humanity, and may be able to do something towards realizing the purposes. Jesus was a pioneer in this field, and his followers become more fully sons and daughters of God as, following him, they understand God's purposes more fully and seek to realize them. It might even be suggested that in so far as one comes to understand God's purposes and is committed to realizing them one enters into a sphere above the noosphere, perhaps to be called the theiosphere, and Jesus would then be regarded as the one who first found the way into this.

This discussion has been more concerned with divine sonship than with the conception of man as God's *khalīfa*. There are similarities between the two conceptions, but also differences. So far Muslims have done little to work out all the implications of being God's *khalīfa*, though generally accepting this interpretation of the Qur'ānic passage. Until Muslim thinking on this matter has developed further, it would seem premature to say anything more about it here.

(d) Towards fuller freedom

The freedom of the human being according to the common sense view is no more than the lowest level of freedom. Beyond that I must endeavour to escape from the constraints placed upon me both by my own individual being and by distortions in my social milieu. The constraints caused by ignorance are to be lessened by trying to gain fuller and more accurate information and knowledge. The constraints caused by individual neurotic tendencies can be overcome in so far as the individual is able to bring to consciousness the repressed contents underlying the neuroses. This may be done either by formal psychoanalytic methods or by less formal methods in which there may be a religious element.

The greatest constraints on individual freedom are those due to the distortions in one's socially constructed view of reality, and these are the most difficult to deal with. Such constraints are possibly included in Paul's list in Ephesians 6.11 f.:

> Put on God's armour so that you may be able to stand against the wiles of the devil; for we wrestle not against flesh and blood, but against principalities, against powers, against the rulers of the darkness of this world, against spiritual wickedness in high places.

The central difficulty is that we live, as it were, enclosed within this view, and that all our perception of reality is coloured by it. Fortunately there are one or two loopholes. If we become friendly with someone from another cultural background and appreciate his point of view, this may make us aware of some of the distortions in our own view of reality. This is one of the great gains we receive from dialogue with other religions. The other main possibility is that God may speak directly to us by an 'inner prompting'. This is most likely to happen when we have meditated deeply on our own religious tradition. There is a sense in which the Christian who is familiar with the Bible and meditates on it is placing himself in a different cultural context, and so reaching a standpoint from which he can criticize his own society's view of reality.

People approach this fuller freedom, however, only in so far as they are committed to serving God and seeking to do his will and fulfil his purposes. This also implies some further acceptance of responsibility. The person who has become aware of neurotic tendencies in himself and is no longer dominated by them will now say, 'Yes, I did that', even though when he did it his motivation was unconscious. A more important extension of responsibility, however, is when the person becomes more fully identified with the purposes of God. Dag Hammarskjöld, just before his election to the second term as Secretary-General of the United Nations, wrote in his *Markings*: 'Your responsibility is indeed terrifying. If you fail, it is God, thanks to your having betrayed him, who will fail mankind. You fancy you can be responsible *to* God; can you carry the responsibility *for* God?' (3.9.57). There is much truth in this, though one would also have to say that, if there was a failure, it would be only one of the possibilities open to God which remained unrealized, whereas his overriding purposes were not frustrated.

The individual who commits himself to serving God and says 'Yes' to his personal vocation as part of God's purposes, must also in some sense affirm God's purposes for the world as a whole. He cannot follow Omar Khayyam in Fitzgerald's poem and go on thinking that the universe is bad, should be shattered to bits and remoulded on another plan—so as to reduce pain, frustration and other ills. There is a sense in which in willing his own vocation in full freedom he is also willing the universe as it is, with all that makes it 'this sorry state of things'. He has to see the flaws in the cosmic process and yet, despite these, believe that it is good. In short, the fuller a man's understanding of the purposes of God in general, and the fuller his knowledge of himself and his vocation, so much more clearly does he see that his vocation is to act for God in his own special circumstances. To achieve this is to have entered the theiosphere.

(e) Controlling the future

The deepest thinking of Muslims and Christians would agree in holding that humanity never completely loses its creatureliness or servile status. This is contrary to much secular thinking today, which claims that because of the advances in our scientific knowledge we are now able to control the future course of evolution. It is certainly true that human powers are now such that they can greatly *affect* the course of evolution; if we produce a nuclear holocaust, evolution might have to retrace its course from the level of the insects. It is dangerous to suppose. however, that, if we attempt to give a positive direction to the future course of evolution, we are bound to succeed. The truth is rather that we are bound to fail unless our plans are in accordance with the purposes of God—or, if one prefers, with the 'orientation' which is a part of man's nature. If owing to imperfect knowledge or false valuations our plans are not in accordance with the 'orientation' implanted in all creatures, there will be unforeseen repercussions, and the final result will be quite different from what was expected. Future planners should be warned by the ignominious failure of the great

British ground-nuts scheme after the Second World War, which was to solve many of the world's food problems, but which came to nothing because some essential facts had been overlooked.

Not much need be said about controlling the future course of history, which superficially at least is even more difficult than controlling evolution, since countless unpredictable human factors are involved. Despite much lip-service to peace the politicians are far from having produced a peaceful world.

The first priority here is that the politician, however powerful he may be, should remember that he remains God's 'creature' or 'slave', and that his efforts are only likely to be successful in the long run in so far as he has committed himself to trying to realize God's purposes and has developed his inner sensitivity so as to gain a fuller understanding of these purposes.

Chapter 8

Islam and Christianity today

I Contemporary problems and responses

At the present moment the popular mind in the West is very much aware that there is an Islamic resurgence, especially in Iran. This, however, is only a part of the total contemporary meeting of Islam and Christianity, and in order to understand its place in the whole we must look more closely at some features of the background.

During the last two centuries, and especially during the last seventy years or so, the West has made phenomenal advances in science and technology. These have made the West itself a very different place to live in, but their effects on the non-Western world have been infinitely greater. The impact of the West (at first only Western Europe) first made itself felt on the Islamic world in 1498 when Vasco da Gama reached India and opened a new trade route. After a time trade led to political involvement, then to colonialism and other forms of Western control. In the nineteenth century the advance of Western technology made it easier for the Westerners to control great regions of the world's surface; but at the same time it has to be remembered that the wealthier individuals in non-Western countries were eager to acquire the comforts, conveniences and luxuries which the West was now able to supply. Non-Western countries, including Islamic ones, now possess the latest means of transport and communication devised in the West, not to mention many of the products of its military technology. Educational systems based mainly on Western ideas have also been developed in non-Western states, even when formally independent.

In most Islamic countries this acceptance of material goods and education from the West has led to deep internal repercussions. A new social class has emerged consisting of those persons with a Western education or able to handle the products of Western technology. Among the old merchant and land-owning classes those who adopted Western methods (of irrigation, for example) have prospered and grown in wealth and power, while those who remained fixed in the old ways have lost out. The old religious-intellectual class of the ulema or jurists has tended to resist change and as a result its power and influence has greatly declined. Since about 1950 the speed of change has greatly accelerated, and this has left the masses of ordinary people utterly bewildered and feeling anxious and insecure, as they saw the disappearance of familiar objects and ways of acting and their replacement by things strange and new.

It is chiefly out of this feeling of insecurity that the Islamic resurgence or revival has developed. People looking for security think of 'the good old days' when the old religion was properly observed. One aspect of this insecurity is the fear of being, as it were, drowned in Western culture and losing one's traditional identity. Consequently in turning to the old religion they tend to emphasize those features which make it culturally distinct from the West, such as the prohibition of alcohol and usury and the use of the veil and similar coverings by women. To this extent the Islamic resurgence is a reassertion of identity, indeed a reassertion of identity against the West. They suppose that much of the administrative regimentation to which they are now subject is somehow directly due to the West, although it is due just as much to their own acceptance of Western products and to the social and economic changes consequent upon this. While identity is thus vigorously reasserted, however, hardly anything is done to solve the problems created by these social and economic changes.

This very conservative response to the impact of the West is found not only in the Muslim masses but in the corps of jurists or ulema (wrongly called 'clergymen' in the Western media). This type of response can indeed be traced back for centuries. A not so distant example comes from the India of about one hundred and fifty years ago, where the Hindus were eagerly getting Western education for their children, while the Muslims remained aloof; and the not surprising result was that the best government posts open to Indians nearly all went to Hindus, while the Hindus also benefited in other ways. In the Ottoman empire, including Egypt, in the nineteenth century the ulema refused to modify their educational curriculum to include Western subjects and to make permissible changes in the rules of the Sharīʾa to facilitate trade between the Ottoman empire and non-Muslim

Europeans. Up till about 1850 the position was that the powerful and hierarchically organized corps of ulema controlled higher education, the formulation of detailed laws and the administration of justice; but after that date, largely because their extreme conservatism made the sultans bypass them, they gradually lost most of their power until their influence became only a pale shadow of what it had been.

Extreme conservatism is not restricted to Islam but is found also in the West as well as in revival movements in all the great religions. In the West also there is insecurity and anxiety resulting from technological advances and their repercussions, not least the threat of nuclear war and the general erosion of values. Notable among the more conservative responses have been those of what might be called the 'American far right'. It is said that the adherents of the burgeoning revival movements of the 'Bible belt' were an important factor in the election of President Reagan in 1979. Some have gone the length of asserting that the Bible produces a coherent biological theory which they label 'creationism' and see as a counterblast to evolutionism. From the standpoint of this book the supposed opposition between these two 'theories' is, of course, based on misunderstandings.

In contrast to this conservatism there are many Muslims and Christians who have responded more creatively to the contemporary situation. A creative response to his own situation was lived out nearly nine centuries ago by al-Ghazālī, of whom something has been said above (pp. 77f.). Essentially a response is creative when a person, without abandoning any central religious doctrines, tries to effect a degree of harmony between these and the current scientific and philosophical outlook, and in so doing to provide a basis for dealing with social and political problems. A total creative response, of course, such as desiderated here, will often be the work of several or even many people, making different contributions to the whole. Among Christians who have responded creatively are several of those whose thinking has been heavily drawn on in the present work, such as Teilhard de Chardin for evolutionary questions and Thomas Merton for more practical ones. Among Muslims the greatest names of the recent past are those of Muḥammad 'Abduh and the great Iqbal; but since these and up to the present time there are countless others who are working away steadily at various aspects of the total response needed. They seldom reach the headlines, but nevertheless in the end their work will be more fruitful than that of most of those who do. It is such persons who will be most active in dialogue with non-Muslims, and it is from their number that the true leaders of Islam in its fifteenth century will come.

II Continuing the dialogue

As I look back on this book I find that I have tended to emphasize the similarities between the two religions, although this was not consciously any part of the original plan. I have come to believe, however, that one cannot defend belief in God in the present age without giving much thought to what I have called 'the symbolic use of language', and further that, when one appreciates the fact that symbols which appear contradictory are not necessarily so, many of the differences between the religions fall away. Between Islam and Christianity, however, there remain many differences of emphases and also one or two more fundamental differences. In a long article of mine on Muslim-Christian dialogue published by a Muslim friend, Hakīm Muhammad Said, in the periodical he edits,[1] I spoke of several points which would have to be considered in future dialogue. Here I want to focus attention on the area where, as I see it, the main difference between Islam and Christianity is to be found. This is that, because Muslims have not accepted the historical fact of the crucifixion of Jesus, they have failed to understand most of the Christian teaching about the meaning of his death and resurrection and the nature of his work of 'salvation'.

By the standards of modern historiography the crucifixion of Jesus is one of the most certain events in past history, as certain—dare one say it?—as the fact that Muḥammad proclaimed the religion of Islam in Mecca about the year 610 (a fact which has been implicitly denied in some recent books, though on wholly inadequate grounds). Although the crucifixion appears to be denied by the Qur'ān, the passage (4.157-9), when looked at in an eirenic spirit, is not as decisive as has commonly been thought by Muslims. It asserts that the Jews 'did not kill him, did not crucify him', and this is true in the sense that it was not the Jews who did it but the Romans (though following on his condemnation in a Jewish court). It is also true that the implicit suggestion in the Jewish claim, namely, that they had been victorious over Jesus and his followers, is completely false, as is shown by later history. Then there is the phrase *shubbiha la-hum*, 'it was made to appear to them', which can be interpreted in many different ways, not all of them contrary to Christian teaching. Some Muslims are coming to realize that there is a problem here with which they will have to grapple sooner or later. An interesting attempt to do so has been made by Mahmoud Ayoub in an article entitled 'The Death of Jesus, Reality or Delusion'.[2]

With regard to the 'salvation' achieved by the crucifixion and resurrection of Jesus, or his 'saving' of the world, there is no single Christian account. Many different phrases are found in the New Testament. An angel tells Joseph that Mary's son 'shall save his people from their sins' (Matthew 1.21). Similarly, Paul writes that 'Christ Jesus came into the world to save sinners' (1 Timothy 1.15). Jesus himself is reported to have said, 'I came not to judge the world, but to save the world' (John 12.47). Several times he is spoken of as 'saviour', and through him or through 'his name' (Acts 4.12) 'salvation' is said to come. Another term used is 'redeem', which has the connotation of freeing someone from slavery. Jesus is called 'redeemer'; and Paul speaks of our having 'redemption through his [Jesus's] blood, the forgiveness of sins'.[3] Yet another conception is that 'God was in Christ reconciling the world to himself' (2 Corinthians 5.19). There are still other phrases that could be mentioned, but it is pointless to do so, since all require interpretation and there is no agreement among Christians about the interpretations. A completely different way of describing the achievement of Jesus (or the 'salvation' he achieved for us) was that given above, namely, that by gaining insight into the principle of the conquest of evil by love and by living it out he opened the theiosphere to his followers.

To say that Muslims have failed to appreciate Christian teaching on such matters is not to say that there is nothing comparable in the thinking of Muslims. It is possible that not much is to be found in the main stream of Sunnite thinking, for there has even been little discussion of the sacrifice which is made in the course of the Ḥajj. Ṣūfī writers, however, have explored neighbouring fields to those to which so much attention has been given by Chrstians; and in Imāmite Shī'ism the martyrdom of Ḥusayn has been a focus for profound reflection on the mysteries of love and suffering. Mahmoud Ayoub (mentioned above) has made an important contribution to scholarship and dialogue alike with his book *Redemptive Suffering in Islam: a Study of the Devotional Aspects of 'Āshūrā' in Twelver Shī'ism* (The Hague, 1978). In the future there will doubtless be more such books by Muslims from a variety of backgrounds.

In this world in which there are increasing contacts—many of them very friendly contacts—with followers of other religions it is the duty of every believer both to improve his understanding of his own faith and also to try to gain a fuller positive appreciation of other faiths. There is no question in the foreseeable future of any amalgamation of religions, however, The first stage would rather be that of mutual recognition where the various world religions accept one another as fellow-climbers of the cloud-covered mountain on whose summit in the mists God dwells unseen.

Notes

Abbreviations

EI[1], *EI*[2]: *Encyclopaedia of Islam*, first, second edition. (Some articles of the First Edition are also in *The Shorter Encyclopaedia of Islam*)
S.: Sura (chapter of the Qur'ān)

1 Attitudes and approaches

1 E.g. 5.44–8; cf. W. M. Watt, *Islam and the Integration of Society*, London, 1961, 267–9.
2 E.g. 2.135, 140; 3.65–8.
3 Watt, *Integration*, 260–5 with further references.
4 Cf. Adel-Théodore Khoury, *Polémique byzantine contre l'Islam (VIIIe–XIIIe S.)*, Leiden, 1972.
5 Cf. Normal Daniel, *Islam and the West: the Making of an Image*, Edinburgh, 1960; W. M. Watt, *The influence of Islam on Medieval Europe*, Edinburgh, 1972, esp. 72–7.
6 W. M. Watt, *The Faith and Practice of al-Ghazālī*, London, 1953, 20.
7 *Conjectures of a Guilty Bystander*, New York, 1968 (paperback), 144.

2 The affirmation of religious truth against scientism

1 In *The Social Construction of Reality: a Treatise in the Sociology of Knowledge* (1966); quoted from the edition in Penguin University Books, Harmondsworth, 1971.
2 Op. cit., 33 (italics mine).

3 The original American edition of 1967 was entitled *The Sacred Canopy*; the quotations are from the edition in Penguin University Books, Harmondsworth, 1973, 25, 29.
4 *Social Reality of Religion*, 33.
5 Ibid., 19.
6 Ibid., 34.
7 *The Foundations of Belief*, London, 1969, 139–57.
8 Cf. *Discours de la Méthode*, Part III.
9 *The Self as Agent*, London 1957, 21 f.
10 William James, *Pragmatism*, London, 1907, 234, remarks: 'Schiller says the true is that which "works" . . . Dewey says truth is what gives satisfaction.'
11 Tillich, *Systematic Theology*, i, Chicago, 1951, 102; cf. 105.
12 Matthew 7.15–20.
13 Qur'ān, 4.13; 5.19; 9.72, 89, 100, 111; etc.
14 Andrew Greeley, *Unsecular Man*, New York, 1974, esp. ch. 4, 84–124. Contrast the discussion in Britain about John Hick (ed.), *The Myth of the Incarnate God*, London, 1977.
15 *Does God exist?*, London, 1980, 639.
16 The use of the word 'pattern' is explained in section III(d) below.
17 By Stephen Toulmin and June Goodfield, London, 1962, and Harmondsworth, 1965.
18 Cf. Michael Polanyi (with Harry Prosch), *Meaning*, Chicago, 1975, 75–81; also I.A. Richards, *Principles of Literary Criticism*, New York, 1942; Max Black, *Models and Metaphors*, Ithaca, N.Y., 1962.
19 I. Progoff, *The Symbolic and the Real*, New York, 1973 (paperback), 95 f.
20 W. M. Watt, *Truth in the Religions*, Edinburgh, 1963, 111–17.
21 In Roland Robertson (ed.), *Sociology of Religion: Selected Readings*, Harmondsworth, 1969, 262–92, esp. 263, 267 (reprinted from *American Sociological Review*, xxix (1964), 358–74).
22 Ibid., 268.
23 Cf. Isidore Epstein, *Judaism*, Harmondsworth, 1959, 80 f.
24 Cf. C.G. Jung, The Archetypes of the Collective Unconscious (*Collected Works*, vol. 9/1), London, 1959, index.
25 John 1.18; 1 John 4.12; 1 Timothy 6.16.
26 Exodus 33.18–23.
27 Isaiah 6.1–10.
28 Job 42.5 f.
29 1 Corinthians 13.12.
30 Quoted in Basil Willey, *The Seventeenth Century Background*, Harmondsworth, 1962, 157.
31 Al-Ghazālī in Watt (tr.), *Faith and Practice of al-Ghazālī*, 23.
32 *Discours de la Méthode*, Part 4, ad init.

33 Michael Polanyi, *Meaning*, 25.
34 Polanyi, *Knowing and Being*, ed. Marjorie Greene, Chicago, 1969, 219.
35 Cf. Karl Stern's treatment of Descartes in *The Flight from Woman*, New York, 1966, 75–106.
36 'Christianity and the non-Christian Religions', in John Hick and Brian Hebblethwaite (eds), *Christianity and Other Religions*, London, 1980, 52–79.
37 *Knowing and Being*, ch. 14, 'Life's Irreducible Structure', 225–39.
38 Ibid., 225.
39 Ibid., 233.
40 Ibid., 234.
41 Ibid., 238
42 In Watt, *Islamic Revelation in the Modern World*, Edinburgh, 1969, 30–6, an attempt was made to state categorial differences between the Arab mentality presupposed in the Qur'ān and that associated with the English language. See also below, ch. 4, p. 62.
43 *Meaning*, 32–5 and index.

3 The names and attributes of God

1 Edited by Annemarie Schimmel and Abdoljavad Falatūrī, London, 1979; original German, Freiburg i. B. 1975.
2 E.g. 10.18; 29.61–5; 39.2, 38; etc. Cf. W.M. Watt, 'Belief in a "High God" in pre-Islamic Arabia', *Journal of Semitic Studies*, xvi (1971), 35–40; 'The Qur'ān and Belief in a "High God"', *Der Islam*, lvi (1979), 205–11. Cf. Psalms 16.2f., as interpreted in the Jerusalem Bible.
3 *The Koran . . . translated into English*, Preliminary Discourse, section 4, ad. init. (there are many editions).
4 English translation, *Mohammed the Man and his Faith*, revised edition, New York, 1960, 25, etc.
5 *Al-Maqṣad al-asnā fī asmā' Allāh al-ḥusnā*, various editions. The relevant section is translated by Richard J. McCarthy in his *Freedom and Fulfilment*, Boston, Mass., 1980, 340–7; it is not included in the partial translation by Robert Stade, *Ninety-nine Names of God*, Ibadan, 1970.
6 Cf. *EI*², art. (al-)Asmā' al-Ḥusnā (Louis Gardet).
7 Acts 11.15.
8 Cf. C.C.J. Webb, *God and Personality*, London, 1918.
9 Cf. W.M. Watt, 'The Christianity criticized in the Qur'ān', *Muslim World*, lvii (1967), 197–201; also Geoffrey Parrinder, *Jesus in the Qur'ān*, London, 1965.
10 Georg Graf, *Geschichte der christlichen arabischen Literatur*, ii,

Vatican City, 1947, 236; cf. Paul Sbath, *Vingt Traités philosophiques et apologétiques d'auteurs arabes chrétiens*, Cairo, 1929, 12.

11 Cf. Sbath, *Vingt Traités*, 104, 109.

12 *Al-Milal wa-n-niḥal*, ed. Cureton, London, 1842 (1946), 172; Cairo, 1367/1948, ii.34.

13 For the interpretation see W.M. Watt, *Muhammad at Medina*, Oxford, 1956, 313.

14 Al-Wāqidī, *Maghāzī*, ed. Marsden Jones, London, 1966, 1.191.

15 For references see W.M. Watt, *Bell's Introduction to the Qur'ān*, Edinburgh, 1970, 121–4.

16 Ezekiel 34,11–16; Psalms 23.1; Isaiah 40.11; Matthew 18.11–14; Luke 15.3–7.

17 16.36; 10.47.

4 Scripture as the word of God

1 Majid Khadduri, *Islamic Jurisprudence: Shāfi'ī's Risāla*, Baltimore, 1961, 110–12, also referring to S. 2.129, 151, 231.

2 Cf. p. 18 above.

3 Cf. W.M. Watt, *The Formative Period of Islamic Thought*, Edinburgh, 1943, 284; J.R.Th.M. Peters, *God's Created Speech*, Leiden 1976, 282, 331.

4 Cf. p. 42 above and note 42 to ch. 2.

5 Leslie Dewart, *The Foundations of Belief*, London, 1969, esp. 150–68.

6 Ibid. 133.

7 2.22; 13.3; 15.19; 20.53; 43.10; 50.7; 51.48; 71.19; 78.6; 79.30; 88.20; 91.6.

8 Cf. Watt, *Bell's Introduction*, 48–50.

9 Cf. ibid. 44–7. Ibn-Abī-Dāwūd's *Kitāb al-Maṣāḥif*, has been edited by Arthur Jeffery in his *Materials for the Study of the Qur'ān*, Leiden, 1937.

10 Ezekiel 24.15–27; S. 93.6–8.

11 For details see my *Muhammad at Medina*, Oxford, 1956, 228–38.

12 Cf. W.M. Watt, *Integration*, London, 1961, 259f.; also 'The Early Development of the Muslim Attitude to the Bible', *Transactions of the Glasgow University Oriental Society*, xvi (1957), 50–62, esp. §1.

13 Cf. *EI*², art. Ḥadīth (J. Robson), esp. section 2.

14 There is a fairly accurate translation of the Nicene creed in ash-Shahrastānī, *Milal*, London, 1842 (1946), 174f; Cairo 1367/1948 (ii.43).

15 Cf. J. Schacht, *An Introduction to Islamic Law*, Oxford, 1964, 62; cf. 19–21.

5 God the creator

1 What follows is based mainly on M. Polanyi, *Knowing and Being*, ed. Marjorie Greene, Chicago, 1969, ch. 14, and Teilhard's *Phenomenon of Man*, Book I, ch. 3, and Book II, ch. 1.
2 *Knowing and Being*, 227.
3 *Phenomenon*, 68–74, 78, 180–4, etc.
4 Quoted by Theodosius Dobzhansky in John Lewis (ed.), *Beyond Chance and Necessity*, London, 1974, 133, from a paper by R.C. Lewontin.
5 *Chance and Necessity* (paperback), Glasgow, 1973, 151.
6 Lewis (ed.), *Beyond Chance and Necessity*, 133.
7 Dobzhansky, loc. cit.
8 S. Toulmin and J. Goodfield, *The Architecture of Matter*, London, 1962, and Harmondsworth, 1965, 367.
9 Lewis (ed.), *Beyond Chance and Necessity*, 96–102.
10 *Phenomenon*, 65.
11 *Science and Christ*, London, 1968, 211; cf. 193f.
12 *Phenomenon*, 108f.; discussed by Dobzhansky, *The Biology of Ultimate Concern* (paperback), London, 1971, 117–19; also by John O'Manique, *Energy in Evolution*, London, 1969, 68–70.
13 *The Appearance of Man*, London, 1965, 140.
14 Ibid., 139.
15 *Phenomenon*, 237–53, esp. 241, 253; cf. *The Future of Man*, London, 1964, 176f.
16 7.54; 10.3; 11.7; 25.59; 32.4; 50.38; 57.4; 65.12.
17 2.117; cf. 3.47, 49; 6.73; 16.40; 19.35; 36.82; 40.68. There is a comparable but more poetic account of the embryo in Job 10.9–12.
18 Creed attributed to Abū-Ḥanīfa; in A.J. Wensinck, *The Muslim Creed*, Cambridge, 1932, 103.
19 Mark 16.19; Acts 7.55f.; Nicene Creed.
20 Cf. Edward Schillebeeckx, *Interim Report*, London, 1980, 17.
21 Mark 6.35–44; 8.1–10; and parallels.
22 Mark 4.35–41 and parallels.
23 2 Kings 4.42–4.

6 God as the lord of history

1 E.g. *A Study of History*, xii, London, 1961, 218.
2 W.M. Watt, *Formative Period*, Edinburgh, 1943, 105; etc.
3 Cf. his *Contemplative Prayer*, London, 1973, foreword by Douglas V. Steere, 11.
4 Teilhard, *Phenomenon*, 211.

5 Cf. W.M. Watt, *Truth in the Religions*, Edinburgh, 1963, 126f., where the 'diagrammatic' character of ideas is discussed.
6 This is done in Joseph Neuner (ed.), *Christian Revelation and World Religions*, London, 1967, especially in the article by Hans Küng.
7 Cf. Norman Cohn, *The Pursuit of the Millennium*, London, 1957.
8 Cf. *EI*[2], art. (al-)Dadjdjāl (A. Abel); the numerous references in Ḥadīth are listed in A.J. Wensinck, *A Handbook of early Muhammadan Tradition*, Leiden, 1927, s.v. Dadjdjāl.
9 Cf. *EI*[1], art. Shafāʻa (A.J. Wensinck).

7 Humanity in relation to God

1 W.M. Watt, 'God's Caliph', in C.E. Bosworth (ed.), *Iran and Islam*, Edinburgh, 1971, 565–74.
2 Cf. John 15.15; Hebrews 3.5f.; Galatians 4.7.
3 Cf. 1 Corinthians 15.35–44; Philippians 3.21.
4 *Conjectures of a Guilty Bystander*, New York, 1968, 235–9.
5 Exodus 31.13–17.
6 Numbers 15.32–6.
7 37.36; 44.14; 68.2; etc.
8 16.103; 25.4; etc.
9 Details in Norman Daniel, *Islam and the West*, Edinburgh, 1960.
10 Cf. also Galatians 4.7 and Hebrews 3.5f.

8 Islam and Christianity today

1 *Hamdard Islamicus* (Karachi), i (1978), 1–52.
2 'Towards an Islamic Christology, II: The Death of Jesus, Reality or Delusion', *Muslim World*, lxx (1980), 91–121.
3 Ephesians 1.7; cf. Romans 3.24; Colossians 1.14.

Index